TEACH
THEM
diligently

Raising Children of Promise | LESLIE NUNNERY

What others are saying ...

How many generations does it take to lose the culture?

According to the Bible — it only takes one.

In her first book, author Leslie Nunnery shines a much-needed light on the struggle many parents are having to pass on a godly legacy to their children. She gets right to a fundamental weakness of Christian parenting in this post-modern era: we have forgotten the importance and the privilege of parenting children today. Nunnery offers highlights from the cautionary tale of the Israelites' poor parenting to illuminate what is happening today in many Christian homes: though God has given us the tools to teach our children, we often fail to use them.

There is no question that we can trust God to keep His promises, and that we can trust that His directives to parent will produce fruit. If you're longing to see fruit in your parenting, be encouraged! God is still at work. *Teach Them Diligently* will remind you of the blessing of walking alongside this next generation with purpose and integrity — but more than that, Nunnery reminds readers of the privilege it is to influence and train the next generation in righteousness.

> Heidi St. John, MomStrong International Author
> Speaker, Blogger, Executive Director at Firmly
> Planted Family

❖ ❖ ❖ ❖

I love Leslie's focus on discipleship-based parenting and her heart to help parents. As parents, we must first be what we want our children to become, and she nails that. If you are looking for a discipleship-based parenting book, you've found a great one.

> Kirk Cameron

❖ ❖ ❖ ❖

Clarity, vision, promise ... Leslie Nunnery's book, *Teach Them Diligently: Raising Children of Promise*, restores what the Enemy has successfully stolen from many of the sons and daughters of God. Within the pages of this book you will find the biblical principles of godly parenting articulated with refreshing resolve. Put Leslie's superb book in your arsenal of parenting weapons as you take up the noble charge of raising the next generation of kingdom-building saints!

Chuck Black, author of the Kingdom Series, Knight Series, and War of the Realms series

✦ ✦ ✦ ✦

Have you ever wished you could have a mentor come alongside you, put an arm around you, and guide you through the task of parenthood? Leslie Nunnery does just that in her new book, *Teach Them Diligently*. This book is real, honest, and encouraging. Grab a cup of coffee, take a deep, relaxing breath, and get ready to be blessed by this inspiring new book.

Israel Wayne, author of *Education: Does God Have an Opinion?*

✦ ✦ ✦ ✦

Leslie Nunnery has great news for parents in the midst of raising children. This book, *Teach Them Diligently*, offers a solid biblical approach to parenting — one that infuses hope in the heart of every parent. This book will start you thinking about how to apply Scripture to everyday situations as you gently point your child toward a loving God. With biblical wisdom and common sense, Leslie encourages you to embrace the high calling of parenthood. You will find help and practical ideas through the pages of this book.

Connie Albers, author and speaker

✦ ✦ ✦ ✦

Parents today are desperate to help our kids take hold of their faith and live a life dependent on Jesus. With so many teens walking away from the faith, we are learning it's not enough to teach, warn, and restrict. Our kids need to walk alongside us as we teach them to experience the true love of God. This book is the perfect tool to help us navigate the waters of discipling our kids. Through the transparent stories and wisdom of Leslie Nunnery, homeschooling mom of four amazing kids, this must-have resource encourages and equips parents to teach their children diligently through the authentic moments in life.

Kim Sorgius of Not Consumed

✦ ✦ ✦ ✦

As Christian parents, we all desire for our children and teenagers to grow up genuinely loving the Lord and following Him forever. But far too many unfortunate prodigal stories and paralyzing statistics often leave us feeling disheartened, discouraged, and dominated by fear. In her new book, *Teach Them Diligently: Raising Children of Promise*, Leslie Nunnery combats these parenting challenges with biblical hope, encouragement, and faith.

I especially appreciate how Leslie focuses on grace-based parenting, not "sloppy grace" as an excuse for parenting failure, but "solid grace" as God's foundation for obedience and faith — not trusting in our perfect parenting or striving for perfect kid performance; but instead, honestly believing God's Word, and placing our total faith in our perfect God. We realize we're not saved by works, and our kids aren't saved by perfect parenting; but we also acknowledge that God's instructions for parents are not just "suggestions" but our real-life how-to manual, written by the Creator of the universe, for the benefit of our families and God's Kingdom.

As mission-minded families, we know "We can only export what we grow at home." If we want to be a part of reaching the world with the Gospel of Jesus Christ, we need to begin by raising disciples within the walls of our own homes — discipling our own kids and being disciples ourselves. *Teach Them Diligently* is filled with practical help and instruction to encourage you to raise your kids to love God and the truth of His Word, based on genuine relationship — not performance or perfection, but knowing the person of God Himself.

Leslie Nunnery is the real-deal — she loves the Lord; she enjoys a God-glorifying life with her husband and children, and she finds direction through prayer — leading others from her knees. When I first heard she was writing a book for families, I was thrilled, as I so greatly respect her as a wonderful woman of God; and as I had the opportunity to read the completed manuscript, I was thankful for her hard work and diligence in providing this wonderful resource.

Ann Dunagan
Speaker/Author of *The Mission-Minded Family*

Encourage others!

Thank you for your time and allowing me to share some insight that has been in my heart for my own family for years. If this book is a blessing to you, would you take a moment and leave a review at Amazon.com, ChristianBook.com, and MasterBooks.com?
It would not only be a blessing for me, but an encouragement for those seeking solutions for their own family!

✦ ✦ ✦

Leslie Nunnery

First printing: March 2018

Master Books®, P.O. Box 726, Green Forest, AR 72638

Master Books® is a division of the New Leaf Publishing Group, Inc.

ISBN: 978-1-68344-113-7
ISBN: 978-1-61458-648-7 (digital)
Library of Congress Number: 2018932785

Cover by Diana Bogardus

Unless otherwise noted, Scripture quotations are from the King James Version (KJV) of the Bible.

Please consider requesting that a copy of this volume be purchased by your local library system.

Printed in the United States of America

Please visit our website for other great titles:
www.masterbooks.com

For information regarding author interviews,
please contact the publicity department at (870) 438-5288.

Master Books®
A Division of New Leaf Publishing Group
www.masterbooks.com

Thank You

Special thanks to my husband, David, who never ceases to amaze me through his love for God, his love and care for our children and me, his wise leadership of our family, and his selfless service of others day in and day out. I thank God for you every single day.

To our children Camden, Payton, Lizzie Gray, and Lila, who are actively taking God's Words and applying them to their hearts and who truly show a growing love for the One who has called them to be His children, too: your love for God and others is a great joy to your daddy and me.

To my parents, Tom and Pat Stultz, there are no words to express my gratitude for the way you modeled godly parenting for Kristin and I. I pray every day that your legacy lives on through our children and countless generations to follow.

To my sister, Kristin, who has always been my idea-bouncer-off-er and dearest friend. I could not imagine anyone I would rather grow up with than you.

And, to the Teach Them Diligently team, you are much more like family than friends. David and I are blessed beyond measure to be able to serve alongside of you.

Contents

Foreword

The book you hold in your hand is the result of many years of God's leading and many individuals pouring their lives into mine. Before I was approached about writing a book on parenting, I had never taken the time to consider just how amazingly blessed our family has been. We have seen God work in all of our lives time and time again. We have had countless mentors who have taken the time to share with us their wisdom and experience, and we have always had access to God's Word, which is the source of all truth. A project I thought would take a few months to complete was actually a lifetime in the making.

It was not too long ago that David and I had the opportunity to fly to Texas for a meeting. On our three-hour return trip, we were seated beside a young couple with an adorable, big-eyed, one-year-old girl in footed pajamas and a big red hair bow. (Yes, we southerners do prefer large hair bows even with PJs when our children are in public.) ☺

As the late evening flight took off, both mom and dad sprang into action. To help their little one stay comfortable and content for the flight, they came prepared with toys, milk, little snacks, and lots of cuddles as they passed her back and forth. Despite how prepared they were to keep her happy, though, she did have a few short episodes of tired frustration, which caused them to be obviously concerned that they were bothering those of us around them. Within a minute or so, however, Mama or Daddy's tender care settled her down, and she was happy and content once again.

As I watched this young family, I thought how similar that scene was to the larger picture of our raising our children. How often do we come at parenting as prepared as we know how to be, only to hold our breath every time our children act out at all? How many of us live in fear that they will do as we hear of so many others doing and wander from their faith when they are older?

How I hope that as you read through the pages of this book, you will be encouraged by the fact that the fear of losing our children is not even discussed in God's Word. Instead, He gives us instructions on how we as their parents are to set them on the way they should go, and He gives us lots of examples of ways we can trust Him to take care of us and those we love. Yes, we live in a fallen world, and sadly people act like fallen people — a lot. Were that not true, we would never see any exceptions to the inspired Proverb in which we are told to "Train up a child in the way he should go: and when he is old, he will not depart from it" (Proverbs 22:6). But all of us truly can take heart that God's perfect plan for our families is that our children will be trained well in their youth, and that when they are old enough to start choosing their own way, they will continue in what they have learned. That perfect will is what we all seek. The One who knows our hearts and our children's hearts best is the One we trust. And it is exploring our role in His great plan for our families that this book seeks to do.

I pray that at the end of our time together, you will feel you have a better game plan for parenting your children the way God intended, and that you have a much deeper trust in Him, confident in His ability to hold them close as they grow. For He is strong and mighty, and He loves them with an everlasting love.

Joining you in this journey,
Leslie

Chapter 1

Parenting: God's Great Mystery?

"I have no greater joy than to hear that my children walk in truth" (3 John 1:4). The heart of most Christian parents yearns to be able to join the Apostle John in this sentiment as they look back over their parenting career. Yet, Satan has effectively denigrated the role of Christian parenting to barely more than a high stakes game of Yahtzee. We roll the dice and see what kind of a score we can muster up.

Is that God's plan for His people, though? Can we not know how to get to what both John and another apostle, Paul, spoke of when they talked of their children in the faith? Has God kept the greatest secret from us, so raising godly children is truly just a game of chance?

Absolutely not!

To make discipleship-based parenting a mystery would be completely inconsistent with the character of God. His ways are perfect, He tells us. His truths stand the test of time. He gave us instructions and principles to build our lives upon, and He gives us all that we need to accomplish what He calls us to do.

So, why are we as Christian parents still uncertain? Why do we live in fear? Why are we losing our children in record numbers? What can we do about it?

Ken Ham and Britt Beemer note in their book *Already Gone* that according to statistics, two-thirds of our children will walk away from their faith, and it is very interesting to note that Sunday school and church attendance are not moving those numbers in the right direction. Quite the contrary. They found that those who regularly attend church and Sunday school are actually MORE likely to walk away from their faith. Have we reached the point of no return as parents? Shall we throw our hands up in defeat and just do our best to plug the holes we see as our children sink deeper into Satan's trap? Is raising godly children truly just a game of slim chances where a few will come out right while two-thirds of them won't?

In His Word, God gives us great insight into how we can remove that chance from our parenting. Moses wrote in Deuteronomy 6:7 that we are to "teach (our children) diligently," and he carefully laid out the blessings that come with following that directive as well as the dangers that come when you don't. When the Israelites received this mandate from the Lord, they were about to finally enter the land that was promised to them so many years earlier. It was critical for them that they pass on to their children all they had seen the Lord do and what they had heard from Him as they left Egypt and while they wandered in the wilderness. In the days ahead, they would be inheriting large and beautiful cities they did not build, houses full of good things they did not work for, and so much more. God was about to bless them beyond measure, but He had expectations that they would pass on all they had seen and learned so they would be able to live peaceably and prosperously in their new land. His promise to them was great blessing for the obedience of walking with Him and teaching their children diligently. Later, in the Book of Proverbs, Solomon in his wisdom tells us to "Train up a child in the way he should go: and when he is old, he will not depart from it" (22:6).[1] In these short passages, we see a mandate with a promise that we can build our parenting careers around. And it is that mandate AND that promise that we are going to dive into in the chapters ahead.

Before we can really look at the "how" we are to prepare ourselves for "what" we are to do as parents, we really need to meditate a bit on the "why" we can count on the promised outcome. If we truly trust in the One who made that promise, then we as parents really just need to dive into what it means for us to teach diligently and train up our children in the way they should go — and we should commit ourselves to that task with every fiber of our being, remembering that our responsibility does not lie in the choices of our children long-term. That's between them and God. We are to set them on their way to Him, making sure we put no roadblocks up that would hinder them from knowing and loving Him fully.

So, what does the Bible say about God keeping His promises? Can we count on Him to do so even today?

ABSOLUTELY!

First Kings 8:56 tells us that "there hath not failed one word of all his good promise," and in Romans 4:21, Paul reminds us that we can be "fully persuaded that, what he had promised, he was able also to perform." There is no doubt that God is a promise-keeping God, and that He is able to do all that He says He will. Throughout Scripture, we are reminded that there is nothing too hard for the Lord and that He always keeps His promises. From allowing an old, barren woman to conceive and bear a son, fulfilling a promise made to Abraham many years earlier, to never allowing a widow and her son to run out of oil and flour after she shared her last bit with Elijah, we see a God who is faithful to do what He says He will. The writer of Hebrews tells us in chapter 6 that it is "impossible for God to lie" (6:18) and that through Him we have hope as an anchor of our soul.

A mere 28 years or so after Moses gave the Teach Them Diligently mandate to the children of Israel, Joshua reminded them that God had been faithful to all His promises. Joshua, who had been leading them since Moses' death, notes in his farewell address: "And ye know in all your hearts and in all

21

your souls, that not one thing hath failed of all the good things which the LORD your God spake concerning you; all are come to pass unto you, and not one thing hath failed thereof" (Joshua 23:14). Joshua continues, though, to warn them that if they break their covenant with God and follow after other gods, their destruction is sure to follow. Joshua encourages the people to choose whom they will serve, and with one voice, they announce their choice to serve God. They proclaimed and gave Him honor for what He had done in their sight, even though none of them except Joshua and Caleb had actually seen those works firsthand.

Sadly, Joshua's warnings about what would happen if they were to break their covenant with God came true very shortly after his death. After Joshua and the elders of Israel passed away, another generation rose up "which knew not the LORD, nor yet the works which he had done for Israel" (Judges 2:10). And they did evil in God's sight. Astonishingly, just one generation who did not teach their children diligently fundamentally changed the course of history for the children of Israel, and that fact should get all of our attention.

There is no question that we can trust God to keep His promises, and that we can trust that His directives for parenting are for the good of our families and the furtherance of His kingdom. Parenting God's way will ensure that God's kingdom goes forward and blessing will be upon His people. It just takes one generation to drop the ball, though, before we start to see our children walking away because they do not know God. Let us not be that generation! Let us rise up as parents to teach our children diligently and trust His promised blessing as the outcome.

A.W. Pink once noted, "Faith is not occupied with difficulties, but with Him with whom all things are possible. Faith is not occupied with circumstances, but with the God of circumstances."[2]

❖ ❖ ❖ ❖

Before we move on to the next chapter and embark on the rest of the book, I encourage you to take a few minutes to meditate on the absolute trustworthiness of our great God. Remind yourself that what He promises, He is able to fulfill, and that no problem, no circumstance, no barrier, no past decisions, and no issue is too hard for Him. You may want to do a topical study on faith, the promises of God, or how trustworthy God is to help you focus your heart and mind on the One who created your family, gave you your precious children, and called you to serve Him as their parents. Commit yourself to the task of parenting them with every ounce of your being, and promise with Joshua, that "as for me and my house, we will serve the LORD" (Joshua 24:15).

Endnotes:
1. Unless otherwise noted, all Scripture is from the King James Version (KJV) of the Bible.
2. Arthur W. Pink, *The Life of Elijah* (Morrisville, NC: Lulu Press, Inc., 2017). Kindle edition.

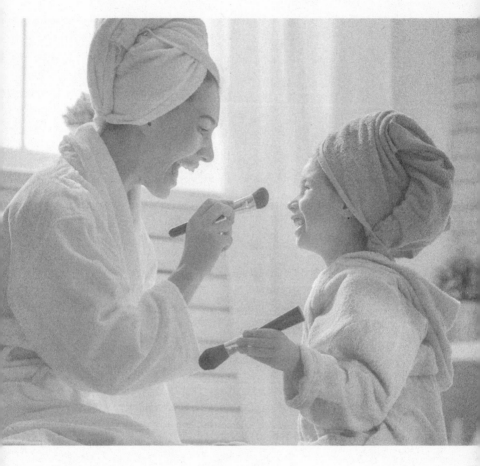

Chapter 2

The Privilege of the Position

> "The thing about parenting rules is there aren't any. That's what makes it so difficult."
> — Ewan McGregor, actor

> "No matter how much time you spend reading books or following your intuition, you're gonna screw it up. Fifty times. You can't do parenting right."
> — Alan Arkin, actor

> "I don't know what's more exhausting about parenting: the getting up early, or acting like you know what you're doing."
> — Jim Gaffigan, actor and comedian[1]

Sadly, these quotes, intended to be cute and funny, actually give us a good idea of how the role of parenting is viewed in our world today. We have lost the sense that "The hand that rocks the cradle rules the world," as was so beautifully noted in the poem by William Ross Wallace.[2] As a society, we have replaced that elevated position of parenting with that of a zookeeper, and tragically that same mindset has become prevalent among Christians as well.

God's families must combat that worldview by building our lives and our families on the Word of God and the truths God has given us. We must see our job as parents as just that — a job God has given us to do. And we must approach that job with more diligence and preparation than any other position we hold, for our success in the job of parent has much higher stakes than any other job we will ever do. But that position also holds greater benefits than any other we will ever enjoy.

In every career you embark upon, you have a set of duties and jobs you are expected to fulfill. For those who love what they do, those duties and jobs bring great contentment and joy. Have you ever stopped to consider all the amazing duties that fall within your job description as Mom or Dad? As parents, we get to do some pretty amazing things with our children, and I'm not even talking about the fun we have, the company we enjoy, or any of the other physical blessings from having our house full of children.

First and foremost, we are called to love our children. One of the directives older women are given is to teach younger women to love their children. One would think that would come naturally to us moms, and to a large degree it does. But, the fact that older women are told to teach us how to do it indicates that there is a love that is much deeper, much greater than anything we humans are capable of without conscious effort and work. This love will prove to be sacrificial from the first day we welcome our child to the world. That love will require daily devotion and humility as we watch our children grow and develop with the hope of eventually seeing them spread their wings to follow God wherever He may call them. That love will make us lose sleep on their behalf, meet physical needs, talk with, pray for, and even worry about their well-being. That love is an incomprehensible love given by God Himself as the greatest tool we have in carrying out every other element of our job as parents. What a tremendous privilege!

We are instructed to teach our children. We are privileged to be the go-to place for answers where our children are concerned. The "whys and wherefores" of the world they live in are learned from their mom and dad. How amazing is that?

Deuteronomy 6 tells us to teach our children diligently about things of the Lord, so they will always know the answer to why things are the way they are or why they happened the way they did (Deuteronomy 6:7 and 20). But we are not only given an incredible opportunity to teach them diligently in the ways of the Lord, but we are also given the chance to teach them diligently about all other things as well. Where do children learn their colors? Generally, through conversations with their parents. Where do children learn their ABCs? Most often by singing a little song with their mom and dad. The list of things we are privileged to teach our children is endless: how they think, what they know, how they interact with others, how big their view of the world is. All of those things and more are an offshoot of the teaching they receive from their parents. I stand in awe that God has given me such a high role, don't you?

We are also privileged to train our children. How is this different from teaching them, you ask? It goes deeper. Instead of simply teaching them facts, theories, truths, and so on, we are commanded to point them in the direction they should grow. We, as parents, are the single biggest influences in our children's lives, so their personality, their direction in life, their drive, their character, and more is shaped through their relationship with us. When Solomon directed us to "train up a child in the way he should go," he was giving us a really big responsibility with a really big reward — "when he is old, he will not depart from it" (Proverbs 22:6). This is a concept we'll explore in much greater detail a little later.

As parents, we are also modeling what a true follower of Christ looks like for our children, and they are like little sponges taking everything in and wanting to be just like us. This point was made very clear to me when my older daughter, Lizzie Gray, was but a toddler. As so many have before me, I walked into my bathroom to find my darling little girl covered in makeup. Black mascara had been smeared all over her face, along with a combination of other powdered colors she had found in my makeup case. She looked at me proudly, exclaiming, "I look just like you!" After my emotions shifted from horror to amusement, I was struck by the significance of that moment. She clearly had no formal instruction in how to properly apply makeup, yet she had such a desire to emulate me that she did what she could. So it is as our children are growing up. Even before they are old enough for deep conversations about the fine points of our faith, they are seeing faith in action through the lives of their parents, and they will try to model it. How often have your children done or said something based on what they have heard you do or say that was so completely out of context you found yourself embarrassed or trying to explain yourself? That's the equivalent of Lizzie Gray's makeup adventure showing up at your church, for our lives provide a walking example for our children to follow day in and day out. And follow us they will.

Next, we have the job of providing for our children. Think of that. When our children are born, they are completely unable to survive in this world. They cannot provide one single thing for themselves. But they are placed in the loving arms of Mom and Dad, and a long-term relationship of trust and provision begins. That child has no choice but to rest in the confidence that Mom and Dad will be there when they need them to be, giving them food, shelter, warmth, clothes, love, and meeting every other physical and emotional need they may have. Second Corinthians 12:14 tells us that it's a parent's job to provide for their children, and as parents we can always trust the Lord to make a way for us to do just that.

We are called to nurture our children. Ephesians 6:4 and Colossians 3:21 make it very clear that we are not to provoke our children, but we are "to bring them up in the nurture and admonition of the Lord" . . . "lest they be discouraged." When we nurture our children, we have the incredible opportunity to give them everything they need to grow, develop, and flourish into the young men and women God created them to be instead of the rebellious, bitter teens our culture has convinced us is inevitable.

We must responsibly lead our children. It seems that the "zookeeper" mentality we looked at when we started this chapter is not a new way of thinking after all, for throughout the New Testament, Paul notes that those who are serving God must have rule over their own houses as well. But that directive is not exclusively for pastors, elders, and deacons. As believers, we must give sufficient attention to directing that which goes on in our homes. We are largely responsible for instilling discipline, work ethic, modeling self-control, and giving our children a solid foundation to stand on before they launch out into the world of adulthood. That is the polar opposite of merely hanging on for dear life and holding down the fort for 18 years.

Because we know them best, we are called to pray for them the most. In Lamentations 2:19 we are told to "lift up thy hands toward him for the life of thy young children." Yes, God already knows what our children need, but through praying for them, God shows us parents what our children really need and allows us to come to know them even better. It's an amazing gift to be able to lift our children before the God who loves them more than we ever could and have Him direct our paths as we fulfill all these other duties for them. By praying specifically for them, God also gives us great insights into their hearts, which allows us to teach and train them much more effectively. He shows us what their needs really are, which helps us as we provide for and nurture them. He helps us see their natural inclinations and fears, which helps us know how to approach them. It is through following the directive to pray for our children that we can most effectively parent them.

Can you believe we get to do all that? I defy you to find another job that offers such a cool set of duties — and I haven't even discussed the pay and fringe benefits that come with our position. We truly are most privileged to be able to call ourselves parents.

❖ ❖ ❖ ❖

In the next section of this book, we will be investigating how we as parents should be preparing ourselves to tackle all these responsibilities we have. But, before we do, why don't you take a few minutes to stop and thank God for the privilege of your calling to be a parent? Do you need to confess an attitude that may have been influenced by the prevailing view of parenting in our culture? Talk to God about that now, and ask Him to give you a vision of what His plans for your family really are. Ask Him to make you the parent He created you to be.

Endnotes

1. http://www.momtastic.com/parenting/541137-40-amazing-quotes-parenthood/.
2. H.D. Northrop, *Beautiful Gems of Thought and Sentiment* (Boston, MA: The Colins-Patten Co., 1980), http://www.potw.org/archive/potw391.html.

Chapter 3

Preparing the Parent

W hat do you want to be when you grow up?"
We start asking that question of children at a very young age. It's cute to hear them speak of their dreams of being a firefighter, doctor, teacher, superhero, etc. As they get older, though, that question starts taking on more importance.

I often sit with my older children, talking to them about what they feel God is calling them to do, what has He put into their hands that He expects them to refine for His service, etc. I am now playing the role of counselor as I help them determine what course of study may be required to better prepare them for the calling God has given them for their lives and what that next step may be. We are prayerfully considering colleges, courses of study, and more as they prepare to spread their wings and seek God's will in the next phase of their lives, and we are explaining to them the stewardship involved with considering all that God has given them, building on those things, and giving them back to Him as the offering of their lives.

None of us set out in our careers with no training or direction, though, do we? Of course not. Quite the contrary is true in most cases as many of us labored through years of schooling, internships, low-level positions, and more, just to have the privilege of being considered for the actual position we really wanted all along. We study. We read. We practice. We endeavor to be the best in our field.

Why don't we view our call as parents in the same way? Why are we not spending at least as much time preparing ourselves for that position as for others? After all, parents hold the most important position of all, for it is the one that can truly affect the course of eternity for many.

When David and I were dating, the Lord led us to a wonderful church outside of Atlanta, Georgia. God used the influence of the pastor and other families there profoundly in our lives as we watched and listened to try to learn everything we could about what the Bible says regarding marriage, parenting, discipleship, and more. By observing the families in that church for the first seven years of our marriage, we felt we were leaving with a much better understanding of what God wants for His people than when we arrived. We have thanked God repeatedly through the years for leading us to Berean Baptist Church when He did, and allowing us to serve there for as long as He did.

One of the big takeaways from our pastor at that time was that "we teach what we know, but we reproduce who we are." To be quite honest, I don't remember the exact context in which he said that, nor do I remember if that was even a main point he was trying to make or simply something said in passing. But it was the main point God had for us, and He has used that point as a reminder for David and me throughout our parenting career.

If we teach what we know but reproduce who we are, it is imperative that WHO we are is WHAT we would want to reproduce in our children. Moses certainly had that in mind as he was giving the last of his expositions to the children of Israel at Mount Horeb all those years ago. As final preparations were being made for the children of Israel to enter the Promised Land and Moses knew he would not be going with them, it is very interesting how he chose to begin those final instructions.

After briefly recounting what God had done since they left Egypt, in Deuteronomy 4 Moses begins talking to parents about how they should live and how they should raise their children. In verse 9, they are told to "take heed to thyself, and keep thy soul diligently, lest thou forget the things which thine eyes have seen, and lest they depart from thy heart all the days of thy life."

Isn't it interesting that he started there? He didn't begin by telling the warriors how to fight or by setting a strategy for taking the land. He didn't talk to the priests about continuing the traditions that had been laid out. No. He started with the family, for he knew that it was the family that would ultimately bring the success or failure of the nation once they reached the Promised Land.

In chapter 5, he reviews the Ten Commandments prior to jumping into a real heart-check for parents in chapter 6. Before Moses tells the children of Israel to teach their children diligently, he talks to parents about examining their own hearts and lives. He offers clear instructions to parents about how they are to be prepared to shepherd the young ones God had given them and to prepare their children to be successful in the land as well.

In the next few chapters, we will be diving into Moses' words in Deuteronomy 4 and 6, to see that he gives expectations for parents before they are instructed to train their children. There is preparation to be made in ourselves before we are fit to take on our "dream job" of teaching our children diligently. We will look at the specific instructions God gave us to make sure we are walking in a manner that gives us the credibility to teach our children diligently. We will see that God has given us the highest and best calling of all, and that He has already equipped us to do exactly what He has called us to do if we are willing to open our hands and give back to Him all that He has given to us. And we will examine the evidences we are to be looking for in our children along the way.

Not long ago, David and I took a short retreat to the mountains. While there, we hiked a tiny bit of the Appalachian Trail. When we stopped at a gift shop in one of the small towns in the area, we saw a t-shirt that cutely read, "I hiked the width of the Appalachian Trail." We giggled, and high-fived that we had, in fact, conquered the width of that mammoth trail. As I walked away, though, I thought about how often we are content to only hike the width of things instead of preparing ourselves to go the distance. How my heart longs for all of us to prepare ourselves so well that we are ready for every stage of our parenting journey. As we grow along with our children, we will see God at work in ways we never dreamed possible, and we will all come closer to Him and to each other. That is God's plan for our families. So, I hope you will jump in with both feet and join me in preparing for that big adventure of teaching our children diligently.

❧ ❦ ❧ ❦

Take a few minutes to prepare your heart for what is to come. It may be that God will point out areas in your own life that need attention. He may require change. Ask the Lord to show you how to prepare yourself to be the exact parent your children need you to be. Ask Him to help you to learn to trust Him to help you become more like Him each day. Commit yourself to tackle more than just the "width" of parenting, but to prepare yourself to go the entire distance, looking unto Jesus for help every step of the way.

Chapter 4

Heart Check: The Fear of the Lord

John Maxwell famously said that "everything rises and falls on leadership."[1] How many organizations, churches, and groups do you know that have fallen apart because those in leadership were unprepared, did something foolish, or simply took their attention off the good of the group and allowed things to creep in that were detrimental to the health of the organization? It happens all the time. Sometimes the fall is great and the collateral damage is extensive and highly visible. Other times, the fall is not as noticeable, but lives are still affected. Naturally, God can override the effects of bad leadership, but often those being led do pay a price for the decisions of the leader. Aren't you thankful that God can fundamentally transform those in leadership through His grace to make them worthy of the position they have been called to hold? WOW! As a parent that makes my heart rejoice, for I know that in myself, my leadership of my children would be futile. It is only through God's strength and by God's grace that I can confidently lead them in His ways.

God's "Teach Them Diligently" mandate begins with some pretty specific directives for parents, a heart-check of sorts, to help us be prepared to lead our children in all of God's ways and to train them to love God with all their heart, soul, and might. His promised blessing will be upon those who obey Him in these ways.

After recounting the great things God had done on behalf of the children of Israel, Moses reviewed the Ten Commandments and reminded the children of Israel to do all that God had laid out for them. He warned them not to add anything to it nor take anything away from it. When we get to Deuteronomy 6, Moses begins by talking directly to the parents and giving them clear instruction about how they are to prepare themselves to parent God's way.

"Thou shalt fear the Lord thy God . . ." (Deuteronomy 6:13).

How curious that the first directive Moses, under the inspiration of God, would give the Hebrews in this passage is about fear. How on earth could fear make them better leaders, better parents, or better followers? As I thought about that, I found that the instruction to fear God showed up quite a bit throughout the Bible.

> Deuteronomy 10:12 — "What doth the LORD thy God require of thee, but *to fear the* LORD *thy God*, to walk in all his ways, and to love him, and to serve the LORD thy God with all thy heart and with all thy soul" (emphasis added).

> Ecclesiastes 12:13 — "Let us hear the conclusion of the whole matter: *Fear God*, and keep his commandments: for this is the whole duty of man" (emphasis added).

> 1 Peter 2:17 — "Honour all men. Love the brotherhood. *Fear God.* Honour the king" (emphasis added).

> Revelation 14:7 — "Saying with a loud voice, *Fear God*, and give glory to him" (emphasis added).

There is no question that God wants His people to fear Him. What does that really mean, though?

That fear of God simply cannot be fear as we generally think of it, for Moses addressed that in Exodus 20:20. When the children of Israel received the law and "saw the thunder-ings, and the lightnings, and the noise of the trumpet, and the mountain smoking" (Exodus 20:18), they were terrified! They begged Moses to speak to them but to never let God do it, for they feared they would die in His presence. Moses comforted them by saying, *"Fear not: for God is come to prove you, and that his fear may be before your faces, that ye sin not"* (Exodus 20:20). And then Moses drew near to that dark (scary!) place where God was. What was the difference between the terrifying fear felt by the children of Israel and the boldness of Moses? Why did the fear of the Lord prompt the children of Israel to draw back, yet it propelled Moses closer into God's presence?

As I meditated on that question, I remembered a time ear-lier this year when I saw a beautiful wedding picture pop up in my Facebook feed. It was a promoted post featuring pictures of a couple who chose to exchange vows on Mt. Everest. I couldn't resist taking a look, and I was rewarded with not only exquisite photos but also a fascinating story.

Ashley Schneider and James Sissom did not want an aver-age wedding. They were seeking adventure as they started their new life together. Though initially interested in a tropi-cal destination wedding, their photographer convinced them that a wedding at the base camp of Mount Everest would give them the wedding of their dreams. So these avid backpackers spent the next nine months vigorously training and preparing for their big day.[2]

Remembering their story, in light of God's command for us to fear Him but not flee from Him as we see in Exodus 20, started me thinking about why they would boldly take their wedding vows at one of the most treacherous places on earth, a place that has cost the lives of many who had ventured there before them.

The difference between the success of their mission to scale Everest and marry at the top and failure was found in the preparation. They studied the mountain before they went. They trained vigorously for nine months. They surrounded themselves with trained and experienced guides on their journey. Although I am confident they had a healthy respect for the dangers of the mountain, they also could take comfort in their training and preparation and move forward toward the pinnacle.

As I thought about that, I realized that it presented us with a small glimpse of how we can have a proper fear of God. All of us fear the unknown, sometimes to the point of horror or dread. If I was standing at the foot of Mt. Everest right now and being told I had to climb it, I would be horrified. I would know that I wasn't prepared for such a hike. I would fear the animals, the weather, the rocks, the darkness, the physical strain and pain, and a thousand other things my mind would conjure up. I would likely become paralyzed by my fear, unable to move and not even wanting to breathe. I would be a fool to think I would survive Mount Everest without first taking the time to study it and prepare for the trek.

We see a similar reaction from the people of Israel, standing at the foot of the mountain where God had just given them the law. They feared Him greatly. In fact, they were horrified! They backed away, not even wanting to be near Him. But Moses knew Him. Moses had spent time with Him. Moses was comfortable with Him. Moses' reaction to the thundering, lightning, and smoke was very different than that of the rest of the Hebrews, for He knew God was orchestrating those things.

Getting to know God and spending time with Him is the key to a healthy, reverential fear of Him. Moses knew very well what God was capable of. He had already been told to take off his shoes, for he was standing on holy ground before an Almighty God. He had seen God's hand at work in countless miraculous ways, and he even had his own countenance changed by merely being in God's presence. But all those mighty deeds didn't keep Moses away, for Moses knew God's heart behind His mighty deeds. He knew His love for His people and His desire to bless them. He knew that God's ways were best, for how could they not be? And he communicated that to God's people by his words and by his actions. He repeatedly went into God's presence.

Therefore, Moses tells us to fear God — not in a shaking-in-our-boots, full-of-dread kind of way, but in an awestruck, how-could-One-so-powerful-listen-to-me kind of way. We should cultivate hearts that know Him and His ways so well that we are filled with amazement every time He enters our minds, and we should love Him so deeply that we have a wholesome dread of displeasing Him. We should present Him to our children in such a way that encourages them to approach Him with awe and wonder as well — and never to run away in fear.

We also see in Scripture that God's forgiveness is a reason for us to fear Him. The Psalmist tells us in 130:3–4, "If Thou, LORD, shouldest mark iniquities, O Lord, who shall stand? But there is forgiveness with Thee, that thou mayest be feared." The same Hebrew word for *fear* that we see in Deuteronomy 6 is also used here. As a parent, I should be filled with humility and wonder when I consider that I am as flawed and sinful as my children are. We both stand bare before a Holy God who covers us with His love and grace and forgives us to the uttermost. How greatly my fear of God will impact how I interact with my children and what my expectations are of them.

The fear of the Lord should be something that draws others to you. Acts 9:31 tells us that the early church walked "in the fear of the Lord, and in the comfort of the Holy Ghost, [and they] were multiplied." Obviously, walking in the fear of God changed their lives, but it certainly did not keep others away. Quite the opposite was true! The lives of those in the early church actually were used by God to draw many others to Him and multiply their numbers rapidly until the whole world would eventually hear the good news of Jesus. Clearly, a fear of

God is a contagious thing that all of us should want to see pervading our families, and making our children and those around us want to know more.

Mike Bennett, in an article about the "Fear of the Lord: What Does It Mean?" says this about the eternal benefits of the fear of God:

> So, rather than a paralyzing terror, the positive fear of the Lord taught in the Bible is a key element of change. It helps us have a proper, humble perspective of ourselves in relation to our awesome God. It helps us in times of temptation when we need to remember the serious consequences of disobeying God; and it motivates us to become more like our loving Creator.[3]

As our reverential fear of God makes us grow to know Him more and to become more like Him, then we should not only grow enough that we don't cower in terror at the thought of God's judgment and power, but we should actually stand in awe of the fact that the Almighty God loves us, forgives us, desires fellowship with us, and will even use us to accomplish His plan in this world. The awe that we, as parents, develop for our great God will then spill over into the way our children view God, making them secure in His love and care from an early age.

No wonder God starts there as He tells us how to prepare to teach our children diligently!

In later years, the children of Israel would sing Psalm 128 as they ascended the Temple Mount. In that Psalm, we see clearly the promises God gives to those who fear Him: you'll be happy in your work, your wife will blossom, and your children will grow like healthy and fruitful plants. That's good news for our families, isn't it?

✦ ✦ ✦ ✦

So how would you describe your view of and relationship with God right now? If you don't know Him well or stand in awe of who He is, your desire to teach your children diligently will be impossible to achieve. How can we teach what we do not know? Take some time right now to ask God to show you how you can know Him better. Commit yourself to studying His Word and to seeking His face each day. Pray that God will show you ways to model a right fear of the Lord for your children. Now is a great time to find an accountability partner with whom you can talk about all that God is teaching you. Your spouse is a great option, so you can start growing closer to God together.

Endnotes

1. J.C. Maxwell, *The 21 Indispensable Qualities of a Leader: Becoming the Person that People Will Want to Follow* (Nashville, TN: T. Nelson, 1999). Note: This phrase has also been credited to the late Dr. Lee Roberson: "Everything Rises and Falls on Leadership," http://fundamentalbaptistsermons.net/Audio/RobersonLeeEverythingRisesOrFallsOnLeadership.mp3; quote is at the 6:15 mark.

2. https://www.today.com/style/mount-everest-wedding-couple-marries-nepal-base-camp-t111353; http://www.cosmopolitan.com/sex-love/a9620508/mount-everest-wedding/; https://meets.com/blog/en/this-couple-of-lovers-got-married-on-the-very-top-of-everest/; https://www.goodnewsnetwork.org/this-couple-got-married-on-mount-everest-and-the-photos-are-breathtaking/; http://www.charletonchurchill.com/mount-everest-base-camp-adventure-wedding-elopement/; http://www.dailymail.co.uk/femail/article-4481616/Couple-tie-knot-Mount-Everest.html.

3. https://lifehopeandtruth.com/god/who-is-god/fear-of-the-lord/.

Chapter 5

Action Time: Keep His Statutes and Commandments

If you are familiar with the work God has given David and me to do, you will realize that "Teach Them Diligently" is a powerful, well-used phrase around our home. Years ago, when God first called us to start an event that celebrated discipleship-based parenting in home-educating families, He immediately brought those words to mind, and He has built our entire ministry upon them. They are foundational, and they are instructive. When we approach our parenting through the lens of teaching our children diligently to love the Lord their God with all their heart, soul, mind, and strength, we find our way much more clearly laid out.

After Moses told the children of Israel to fear God, he moved right into the next foundational instruction for parents. It was as if he was telling them, "Now that you know God well enough to have a proper fear of Him, the next logical step as you prepare yourself to enter the land of promise and raise your children to love God there is that you will want to keep His statutes and His commandments."

Let's talk about keeping God's commandments first, since that's a pretty clear concept for us. As parents, if we teach our children to follow the rules and then don't do it ourselves, we are seriously undermining our ability to lead them. Our children can easily see through a "do what I say, not what I do" way of life, and that will cause them to not have a very high opinion of the One who set those commandments in place, nor of your authority in making sure they are living by those rules.

We must first deal with the sins that are in our own lives before we can have a solid footing to help our children deal with theirs. We need to live without hypocrisy, striving through the fear of the Lord to please Him in all our ways. We must be humble when we do fall, and talk to our children, when appropriate, about our sin and our sorrow for it. Those times of transparent interaction with them about the things we struggle with, the lessons God is teaching us, etc., are invaluable times of discipleship and relationship-building with our children. They start, though, with a heart that longs to walk in truth and to keep God's commandments as Moses instructed us.

The Apostle John tells us in 1 John 5 that keeping God's commandments is an indication that we are actually the children of God and is an outward display of our love for Him. Modeling right actions and obedience before our children is another powerful discipleship tool. The Psalmist tells us that the one who loves God and seeks Him wholly says, "O how I love thy law!" (Psalm 119:97) and "I will run the way of thy commandments" (Psalm 119:32). Our children know whether the love of God and His law is in our hearts, and that will make an impact on them as they are developing their view of God.

David and I tell our children almost every day that their actions are a clear indication of what's in their hearts. If their hearts (or ours) are set to "love the Lord their God with all thy heart, and with all thy soul, and with all they strength, and with all thy mind" (Luke 10:27), their actions will indicate that. They will obey God and serve others, not out of duty, but out of devotion. The fear of God that we have tried to model for them for years naturally leads to hearts of obedience. We are seeing those hearts developing right before our eyes as they grow and mature, but if we fail to practice what we teach through our actions, we are likely to lose their hearts before all is said and done.

Do you have a heart of rebellion or a heart that loves God wholly? Do you keep His commandments simply out of duty or a desire to look good in front of others, or does your love for and devotion to Him naturally spill over into your actions? You may be able to fool many, but your children will know the answer to those questions. We parents should strive to keep short accounts with God and with our children when it comes to keeping His commandments.

In his directive to parents, Moses also notes that we are to keep God's statutes. We don't use the word "statutes" very often these days, but when we do, we're generally referring to the laws or permanent rules of a state or organization. In the context in which Moses was speaking, though, the word he used was understood to be referring to the laws related to festivals or rituals, all the customs God had set in place for Israel through the years that were designed to form a truly religious people — God's people. The Hebrew nation was completely distinct in that they were known by their fear of the Lord and their observation of His ways and obedience to His will. As they were about to enter the Promised Land, Moses was instructing them to not forget God's statutes, so that they would not lose their distinction once they got settled and their lives were easier.

Moses told them that when they observe God's statutes, and in days to come their son asks, "Daddy, why do we celebrate this?" they would have the opportunity to recount for their children all that God has done. I can envision the sparkle in his eye and the excitement in his voice as Moses tells the parents who were listening:

> Then thou shalt say unto thy son, We were Pharaoh's bondmen in Egypt; and the LORD brought us out of Egypt with a mighty hand; And the LORD shewed signs and wonders, great and sore, upon Egypt, upon Pharaoh, and upon all his household,

before our eyes: And he brought us out from thence, that he might bring us in, to give us the land which he sware unto our fathers (Deuteronomy 6:21–23).

What an incredibly exciting story they had to share with their children and grandchildren. The oohs and aahs it would have evoked from their rapt audience surely would have encouraged the heart of the teller as much as it excited the heart of the hearer.

Moses continued to model for them how they could use that story to teach their children diligently and to let them in on the promise that comes with obedience: "And once He led us safely out, the Lord commanded us to keep all these traditions to help us remember His works and to fear the Lord our God, for our good always. He promised to preserve us alive — even through really difficult circumstances. Thankfully, He's still working on our behalf today, and He promises to continue to bless us as we keep serving Him in this promised land!" (paraphrase of Moses' recounting of their story in Deuteronomy 6:20–25).

Don't you love how he reinforces the idea that the fear of the Lord our God is for our good always? He had already told them that they were about to inherit amazing blessings — cities they didn't build, houses full of good things that they didn't even provide, bountiful vineyards that they didn't plant, and enough great food to make them full. All of those blessings were a result of obedience and following after God, and all of those will be part of the life their children will be enjoying in that Promised Land when parents are telling their stories to give their children an idea of why they were experiencing the blessings they were able to enjoy.

Clearly, the story of Israel's escape from Egypt and all their feasts and sacrifices are not part of the heritage of our families. But that doesn't mean that we shouldn't still keep His statutes. That doesn't mean that we don't have fantastic stories and celebrations that can be used to increase and strengthen the faith of our own children — and renew our faith at the same time.

Celebrating what God has done through traditions and keeping His statutes are designed to solicit good questions from our children and serve as great reminders for us. In America, we have a lot of celebrations that can focus our hearts and minds on those things. In our different churches, we have celebrations and remembrances that do the same thing. Even within our individual families, there should be stories of grace that are worthy of telling. How much attention are we as parents paying to them? Do we recognize their value?

I first realized of the value of these celebrations when I was younger and the mission organization my family served with was sending teachers into a land where talking openly about God was not allowed. They were, though, able to talk about American customs, which were of great interest to their students. God worked through those lessons about our traditions, and many students asked questions about them after class when the teachers could more freely answer. Their questions looked very much like what Moses said would happen. "Why do your people celebrate that?" It's amazing how many American holidays can be used as a conduit to share the gospel with others if you are looking for the opportunity to do so.

With that in mind, David and I have been very careful to spend much time talking with our children, using the various holidays and celebrations through the year to point our children to Christ and His love and care for us. But the unique statutes and celebrations God has given to our own family give us even more opportunities to share Him with them. We talk often of the way He miraculously opened doors to lead us to the place we now live. They understand that even as He expected us to take small steps of faith along the way, His power was clearly on display. We talk of the "widow's oil" (2 Kings 4:1–7) He has given us when it looked like we would never have enough money to make it through a month or two, yet in His faithfulness we have never gone without all we need. These and countless other personal accounts of God's goodness, His leading, and His provision for our family give our children a correct view of the amazing God we get to serve.

In our churches, we celebrate the Lord's Supper where we humbly remember the Body and the Blood that Jesus sacrificed for us, and we celebrate baptism, the joyful, public display of those we love to celebrate their new life in Christ. We thank God each week for the fact that we get to worship Him freely with our friends. All of those and so many others are the stories and traditions that fill out the tapestry of grace God is forming within our family.

It's at the conclusion of this point that Moses lays out the first promise that comes with preparing yourself to parent your children God's way: God was about to bless them beyond measure — multiplying them, giving them children, and settling them in a great, bountiful land just as He had told them all those years ago. Their faith, though very weak at times as they wandered in the wilderness, was about to be replaced with a clear view of what God had done on their behalf. They were about to realize exactly what God had promised them years ago, and God wanted to make sure they and their offspring were prepared to enjoy those blessings for generations to come.

✦ ✦ ✦ ✦

So, how are you doing with this part of God's parenting mandate? It's pretty amazing how much of His directive is focused on molding parents, so they can in turn mold their children into His image. Are you consistently keeping God's commandments with a heart of love for Him? Are you sharing with your children God's great works in your family and celebrating His works in times past? Are you using those opportunities to point your children to Christ and deepen their love for Him? Take a few minutes now to write down some of your own stories of grace. Spend time thanking God for all that He has done for you and your family through the years. Brainstorm some new celebrations if need be that can become part of your family's tradition in the days ahead.

Chapter 6

Teach Them Diligently: Discipleship-Focused Parenting in Action

You may be wondering what discipleship-focused parenting even looks like. I once heard discipleship explained as "leveraging everything we have learned in Christ, so others can become more like Him." What an outstanding definition, especially in the context of parenting. All of us want to see our children walk with the Lord and to become more like Him than we are. Therefore, it just makes sense that we would want to take all that we have learned and present it to them in a way that will keep them from making the same mistakes we've made, help them see God's hand in everything sooner than we did, instill in them a single focus of loving and serving the God who created them, and so forth.

Recognizing that God can be trusted to keep His promises for our children as given in Deuteronomy 6 and later in Proverbs 22, and preparing ourselves to parent them by learning to fear Him and keep His commandments and statutes leads us to asking, what does "teach them diligently" actually involve, and how can we as parents be sure we are fulfilling this mandate in God's way? The specific words used in those verses give us a great place to start our investigation and conversation that will take us through the next section of the book.

Personally, I love studying words. I love looking deeply into the meaning of them. I love seeing how they would have been used in the time period in which they were written. I love the richness of them, and by studying the words in Deuteronomy 6 and in other passages, I believe we will see a very clear blueprint for how God wants us to parent our children, bringing them up to love the Lord their God with all their heart, soul, mind, and strength.

The Hebrew word translated for us as "teach them diligently" literally means "to whet or sharpen" and conveys the idea of instilling an idea, attitude, or habit by persistent instruction. It's incredibly interesting to note that the only time in Scripture it is translated this way is in this passage. There are eight other occurrences of this particular word in the Old Testament, and every other time, it is used in the context of sharpening a sword or an arrow or being pierced through. Teaching our children diligently, then, has much more depth of meaning to it than a simple reading through Moses' message may imply.

Let yourself imagine the timing of this mandate. Go back in your mind's eye to see the landscape. Stand at the foot of that mountain like the children of Israel would have and take Moses' words to heart. They are within weeks of taking the Promised Land. They are probably a little nervous about it, many remembering what had happened the last time their people stood poised to take the land and the dangers they were told awaited them there. They didn't know what to expect, but they knew they had to be ready to follow God if they wanted to succeed. They didn't yet know what His battle plan would be, but they knew that the land was filled with people who would not be happy they were marching in. In their heart language, Moses was telling the children of Israel that they were to sharpen their children as they would sharpen a weapon for war, hunting, or protection. Through diligent effort, they were to be making them fit for service and ready to follow their God into the battles to come.

When were they to do that? All. The. Time. When they walked around their houses, when they sat down to eat their meals, when they walked into town, when they were working, when they were going to bed . . . I think you get the point. This was a very practical and life-changing mandate, for Moses was instructing them to be incredibly intentional with every interaction they had with their children, hammering into them God's truths at every opportunity until they were sharp enough to be sent out into battle on their own.

At that time in history, the most effective and beautiful of the weapons available was the bow and arrow, according to Elizabeth Fletcher of WomenintheBible.net. In an article about ancient weapons, she notes that the bow and arrow required "superb craftsmanship . . . and the pay-off was in its performance: It out-classed every other weapon available in the ancient world, barring perhaps the sword."[1] So, when Moses was telling the children of Israel to "teach their children diligently" they understood the importance of it. They understood the gravity of it. They understood the privilege of it. They were preparing their children for whatever would come their way. They were giving them a hope of success in the battles that were to come. They were to be working hard to make them a vessel fit for a king. This was a powerful mandate.

I can't help but wonder if the Psalmist wasn't echoing back to this "Teach Them Diligently" mandate when he says in Psalm 127:3–5:

> Lo, children are an heritage of the LORD: and the fruit of the womb is his reward. As *arrows* are in the hand of a mighty man; so are *children* of the youth. Happy is the man that hath his *quiver* full of them: they shall not be ashamed, but they shall speak with the enemies in the gate (emphasis added).

That Psalm is another of the songs of ascents that the children of Israel used to sing as they approached the Temple Mount. It was yet another way they kept God's statutes by rehearsing His truths, reveling in His promises, and reminding themselves of His directives. When they sang that refrain, they undoubtedly remembered that they were to teach their children diligently, sharpening them as arrows, and praising God for the blessings they indeed turned out to be.

The Bible is full of very practical directions for how we can achieve this mandate in our New Testament world, and how we, like the children of Israel, can instill the habits, beliefs, and ideas that will serve them well and keep them walking with the Lord in the years ahead.

➥ ⬳ ➥ ⬳

The constant interaction we are privileged to have with our children was one of the main reasons God led our family into home education. If we are commanded to sharpen and prepare them to be ready for whatever God has in store for them, we believe God wants us to do that in all areas of their life, both practical and spiritual. By looking for them, we have seen countless opportunities to teach our children diligently day in and day out, and the best part is that they generally happen in such natural ways that they are easy, and they actually strengthen our relationships. So, how about you? Have you been taking your call to teach your children diligently seriously enough? Are you looking at every interaction as a discipleship opportunity? Think about the situations that immediately come to mind where you could naturally but intentionally spend time with your children, sharpening them and teaching them diligently. I think you'll be surprised at how many you'll be able to think of!

Endnotes
1. http://www.womeninthebible.net/war-in-the-bible/bow.

Chapter 7

Train Them Up

Most families have certain phrases that they feel like they've said about 10 million times while their children were little. I cannot begin to count the number of times I said to my children, "Obey quickly. Obey sweetly, and obey completely." Or, "Clean up, clean up, everybody, everywhere. Clean up, clean up, everybody, do your share." Or, "You get what you get, and you don't throw a fit." Those phrases were used liberally for many years in our home. But it's pretty amazing to see the fruit of those phrases now that they're older. By focusing on the heart as well as the action of obedience when they were young, my teens now exercise a sweet spirit, even when obedience is the very last thing they want to do, for they have been trained to know that their attitude in obedience is as obvious and as important as the act of obedience.

If you have woven any of these or countless other cute phrases into your parenting, you're probably already practicing the "train up" mandate found in Proverbs 22:6. That is a passage that is often referred to when people are talking about Christian parenting, and for good reason! There is much to learn from that very short verse.

Solomon tells us to "Train up a child in the way he should go: and when he is old, he will not depart from it" (Proverbs 22:6). Sounds great, doesn't it? As I started meditating on that verse, though, I realized just how little faith I had that God would keep that promise. It seems that many feel that if they even SAY "when he is old, he will not depart from it," they may jinx the whole thing and be destined to have children who walk away from God. How can we know? Our children are their own people, right?

Sure. Our children are their own people. They are ultimately responsible for their own choices and decisions. The fact is, though, that God attached an expected outcome to this inspired Proverb, so I must choose to believe it and devote myself to learning how to do my part of the process.

We've already discussed my love of looking at words, so it should come as no surprise that that's where I started in my study of this passage as well. The Hebrew word translated here for us as "train up" simply means "to initiate or instruct a child in the way he should go." That doesn't give us a whole lot more to go on. But looking at it more deeply unveiled some interesting notes that are very helpful as we formulate our plan of action for carrying out the goal of teaching our children diligently.

There is a nuance to this word that some translators render as "in the beginning of his way," indicating that this training should start as early as the child is capable of receiving instruction. Think of a young plant that you put into the ground. Chances are, you will tie it to a stake or some sort of trellis to help it grow in the right direction. That is exactly what this mandate is telling us. We are not training our children in the way they would naturally go; rather, we are setting stakes in the ground and directing them in the way they *should* go. We must start training them early in the way that, because we love them so much, we would have them go.

This training or redirecting must start as early as possible, or it will become much more difficult to change that bent or direction in which they are growing. The good news is that the early training is by far the easiest. Just as a young plant is very easily guided when it's attached to a stake, a young child is more easily directed in the ways of right and wrong.

That is not to say that they will always obey or necessarily agree with your assessment of the situation, but to a young child, the world has far fewer choices than it does for an older one. They can choose to obey and not touch the stove, or they can choose to disobey and reach out to touch it. One choice will lead to pain while the other does not. Their natural tendency may be to want what they've been told they cannot have, but it generally doesn't take them too long to learn the pain that comes with disobeying mama and daddy's commands.

Training children at this young stage takes consistency and is definitely taxing, but it's fairly clear cut. In many cases, Mom and Dad are the only ones who are making an impression on their children at this stage, and the little ones are literally hanging on Mom's and Dad's every word. This is a great time to start teaching them diligently.

The "guides" that we are putting down in the hearts of our children are not necessarily just rules they need to follow. Although rules are certainly appropriate tools to help us direct our children and maintain discipline and order, discipleship takes a lot more than enforcing rules. Actually, many of the best ways we can set a direction for our children are actually incredibly practical and natural.

Many years ago, our family started making a big deal out of the night the kids were able to do their Christmas shopping for each other. For weeks before, they would find ways to earn money, and on the big day, we would all go out after dinner to allow them to find the perfect gift for their siblings and parents. When they were very young, our Christmas shopping excursion took us to the Big Lots down the road, equipped with non-transparent shopping bags to hide their loot while they scurried through the store hiding from the very ones they were shopping for. David would take two of them, and I would take the other two until the time came to switch up partners and start again. We would giggle, run through the store, hide behind displays, and have the time of our lives. They would take turns checking out with their treasures, and then they'd keep them hidden until we got home and they could run off to the four corners of our house to wrap their gifts.

That Christmas tradition, started when they were far too small to understand the significance of it, has fostered some of the most generous hearts I have ever seen. Our children derive great joy from giving to others all year round, and even as teens they plot and plan to find the best gift they can for everyone they love. Through that simple and fun tradition in our family, our children learned and took to heart the truth that it is better to give than to receive.

Some families serve together in church or local ministries, introducing their children to what servant leadership looks like in action. Many will save Christmas cards they receive as a reminder to pray throughout the year for the families represented. Others keep a blessings box, an answered prayer paper chain, or exercise similar ways of tangibly acknowledging God's work in their family. All of those activities and countless others are great ways to start training up your child in the way he should go.

If you did not get an early start on that training and you fear that you have missed your time to set those guides in the ground, don't worry. God is still faithful, and He is much more powerful than your late start. Let's return to our plant analogy for a moment. Although guiding a young plant may be a little easier, that does not mean that redirecting the growth of a more mature plant isn't possible. Quite the contrary! The growth of older plants can be redirected with proper tending. By strategically pruning and fertilizing, a mature plant will grow in the direction its owner desires to see it grow. The same principle can be true of our children. If you are just starting the process of training up your child when he is a bit older, there may be some pruning to be done — cutting off the things that are leading his heart and mind in a direction that he should not go — and you may need to do lots of fertilization — digging into the truths of Scripture to see why God would have him grow that way — but by God's grace you can still see him take root in the fertile soil of God's love and continue in the way he should go.

Another implication of the word translated "train" for us gives us a picture of putting something in their mouths or giving something to be tasted. Remember when your children were very little, and any food you gave them was either pureed or already cut into tiny little pieces for them? That's the picture this word gives us. Just as little ones are fed only tiny bits at a time as they are able to receive it, so we should be guiding our young children and whetting their appetites for the bigger bites that are to come by introducing them to truths, practicing character traits, reading Bible stories, and worshiping together as a family. We should be instilling habits and expectations in them, so that when they are older, they will have an appetite to learn even more, grow stronger in God's ways, and continue on the path they have been set upon.

As parents, we have been given the unique privilege of influencing our children's tastes and habits like no one else can. Setting their taste buds to crave God's Word and His ways should start as early as possible, while they are still easy to train. These early years are also when you as a parent are learning the skills of teaching them diligently, for they will want to be with you while you walk, while you do laundry, while you clean up the kitchen, while you grocery shop, and so on, and they are likely to be peppering you with questions all along the way. Take those opportunities to set them on a course they will not easily depart from when they are older.

After you have started whetting their appetites and training them in the way they SHOULD go instead of allowing them to go the way they WOULD go, you move on to teaching them the *whys* behind it all. Stakes set shallow in the ground do not hold nearly as fast when the plant gets some size on it as those that are set deep. Although "because I said so," is perfectly valid when our children are very young, it is not long before they will want to know a little more than that, and we start to see their hearts and minds expand to accept the truths of Scripture as their own.

When my oldest was young, he started asking me about salvation. He was so young, though, that I was afraid to tell him for fear that he would doubt his salvation one day and turn from the Lord. By God's grace, He put an older mother in my path to tell me that I should never walk away from a conversation about salvation with my children no matter how old. Jesus told His disciples to "Suffer little children to come unto me, and forbid them not: for of such is the kingdom of God" (Luke 18:16). Just like those disciples, I was forbidding my child to come to Jesus. I was standing in His way. Heaven forbid we do that! Our gracious God allowed Camden to continue to seek Him in the days ahead, and I did not stand in the way after that. Even though he was young, Cam had an appetite for the things of God. He had an understanding of God's love for him. He was being trained in the way he should go, and he responded to it by starting to seek God on his own.

As our children have continued to grow, David and I have taken great care to always talk to them about the "whys" behind what we believed. We endeavored to present Scripture as the basis for all of our convictions and practices. We also let our children know when we had rules that were simply a matter of practice and culture, but were not necessarily on the same level as those based directly on Scripture. Without even stopping to consider what we were doing, we were training our children up in the way they should go. We were teaching them the basis for their belief. We were giving them the tools they needed to start setting their own stakes in the ground as they got older.

About this passage, Joseph Benson wrote, "The impressions made in his childish years will remain unless some extraordinary cause occur to erase them."[1] While there have been notable exceptions, where we would look at a family and certainly be amazed that any of their children would ever depart from the Lord, generally speaking, when we spend the time to train up our children in God's ways from a very young age, setting their expectations and whetting their appetites for things of the Lord, when we are growing and changing as God set out in the "Teach Them Diligently" mandate, we should see them hunger for more of what we gave them in their youth and to continue to grow in the way they should go.

✤ ✤ ✤ ✤

In what ways are you training up your children in the way they should go? Have you started putting the stakes in the ground, so to speak, to keep them from going with their natural sinful bent? Are you digging those guides in deep enough, so they will withstand the growth and deeper questioning that is coming? Take a few minutes now to thank God that He has given us the tools we need to train our children up. If you have been negligent in this way, ask for His forgiveness and the grace to start now. You may want to go to your children and let them know that a change has happened in you and you can all start searching out your "whys" together. What a great exercise that would be!

Endnotes
1. http://biblehub.com/commentaries/benson/proverbs/22.htm.

Chapter 8

The Importance of Our Conversations

The plagues . . ."

The seemingly endless study and review of the children of Israel, the plagues, and their time in the wilderness when my youngest was in early elementary school has provided a long-standing joke for our family. Now whenever anyone is asked what they learned in church or through their devotions, the first-response answer is, you guessed it, "The plagues."

How did our family even find out what Lila was studying for all those weeks? Well, most mornings at breakfast and after every church service or Bible study, we all gather to talk about what we learned, what God is teaching us, and how we can apply that to our lives. These conversations hold us all accountable to be growing to be more like Christ, learning more about Him, and changing into His image day by day. It provides a platform for even the youngest among us to share the good news of Jesus and to become comfortable doing so. It is something that our family has done ever since our children were old enough to communicate God's truths to us, and it has provided some of the very best conversations we have ever had with our kids — as well as giving us great insight into their hearts day by day.

These types of conversations are critical as we train up our children in the way they should go. Throughout Scripture, we are admonished to talk to our children about the great works God has done — His mercies, His judgments, His ways, and His commandments — but many have lost sight of the real power in doing so. Once again, the evil one has deceived God's people into believing that outsourcing the training of our children is better for them and that the parent/child relationship is somehow secondary to the teacher, youth leader, or peer/child relationship. Yet, that is not at all what we see in Scripture.

For countless generations, passing down the Words and ways of God through conversation with their children was the only way kids could know those things. As the fathers told their children of the great things God had done, so their children were expected to pass those truths on to the next generation. This provided a sort of cycle of parenting, where God's truths were naturally passed down through the generations. There was no written Bible that was accessible to families, there were only the stories of God's faithfulness and mighty deeds.

In our day, though, we have a complete canon of Scripture giving us all that we need to know God and to make Him known. Yet, having a written Bible — or in many of our families, multiple copies of God's Word — in our homes does not in any way negate our responsibility to talk of God's truths and His ways with our children. Rather, it gives us the best resource to base those conversations on.

The power of God's "cycle of parenting" is clearly evident in passages like Psalm 78. In that chapter, we see God's expectations for parents as well as what happens when parents don't do their job the way He laid out.

The Cycle of Parenting

Great things God has done! Through the ages, God has given us an abundance of reasons to trust Him, ways to know Him, and catalysts to make us love Him more. He continues to act on our behalf and shower His people with love and grace.

In ancient Israel, fathers knew revealed truths about God and the ways He had worked mightily for His people. They told their children, teaching them diligently in His ways. It was expected that children would hear these truths from their parents as they went about their daily routine, so the children learned these truths naturally from their fathers and became personally grounded in them. The logical next step was that they would eventually pass those truths on to their children and the cycle would start all over again.

We see this parenting cycle laid out in Psalm 78: "Which we have heard and known, and our fathers have told us. We will not hide them from their children, shewing to the generation to come the praises of the LORD, and His strength, and His wonderful works that He hath done" (verses 3–4). In the next verse, the Psalmist passes along the command that all these great things that God has done "they should make them known to their children." We as parents are clearly commanded to talk to our kids about all that God has done! This strengthens their faith. This makes God theirs. This gives them a full narrative of the One they can trust wholly and should love with all their heart, soul, and mind.

Have you ever stopped to consider that your relationship with your children will have an eternal impact on their relationship with God? Yes, God can override a bad parent-child relationship, but it is His plan to use that natural bond to further His kingdom, build disciples, and equip the next generation of believers who can take the good news of the gospel to the uttermost parts of the world. Those natural conversations you have with your children about all that God has done both in your family and in the world at large are building their faith and strengthening their resolve to follow Him.

The next verse we come to in Psalm 78 gives us the promise of what happens when parents are passing down their faith to their children in this way. "That the generation to come might know them, even the children which should be born; who should arise and declare them to their children: That they *might set their hope in God*, and *not forget the works of God*, but *keep his commandments*" (verses 6–7, emphasis added).

Oh, the joys and blessings of doing things God's way! By passing down our faith personally, diligently, and faithfully as commanded throughout Scripture, we will start to see our children walk with God.

But the Psalmist also shows us what happened when that cycle was broken, when the truths of God were not passed on to future generations, and it isn't pretty. The generations were noted as being stubborn and rebellious, cowardly, and not having hearts aligned with God's. "They kept not the covenant of God, and refused to walk in his law; and forgat his works, and his wonders that he had shewed them" (Psalm 78:10–11).

Yikes! When we break that natural cycle of parenting that God has put into place, death and destruction are sure to follow.

Sometimes it's easier to recognize the effects of something when we examine something very tangible. We actually find a very similar cycle happening in nature. Let's take the water cycle as our example. What happens when the natural rhythm of condensation, precipitation, collection, and evaporation or transpiration has a break in it somewhere? Let's say there is a long-term drought in a region, and there is no precipitation. Before long, there is no collection, and since evaporation continues, the lakes and streams start to dry up. The next thing you know, the plants have died, meaning that the food and water supply for living things is becoming scarce. Widespread death is the natural result of a break in that cycle.

That's exactly what we can expect when we as parents are not diligently training up our children in the way they should go, passing on to them the truths of God's revealed and natural

Word, and pointing them in a direction in which their relationship with Him will become personal and deep. We will begin to see children walking away from their faith. We will see families being torn apart. We will see sin becoming widely accepted among God's people, all because moms and dads were not faithful in keeping that cycle of parenting alive in their families.

❧ ❧ ❧ ❧

Are you faithfully participating in this cycle of parenting? Whether you are a first generation believer or come from a long heritage of godly men and women, it is imperative that you pass along your faith to your children. Thankfully, this cycle is as natural as it comes, for we as parents should easily be able to talk to our children about these things. We should not have trouble finding the time to concentrate on these conversations, probe what's in their hearts, share what's on ours, and so on. Think about the last conversation you had with your children. Did it fit this bill, or did you miss an opportunity? Ask God to help you be keenly aware of the opportunities He gives you for discipleship, and ask Him to give you the words to say to point your children (and even your own heart) to Him each time.

Chapter 9

Telling Your Story

Now that we've taken a look at the natural cycle of parenting that happens when moms and dads take the time to talk with their children on a regular basis, training them in the ways of God, pointing their hearts to the One who really can make a difference in their lives, let's see if there are any principles within Moses' message to the parents of Israel that can profoundly impact the way we parent our children today. (Hint: There are!)

Not surprisingly, we see the basic conversation within the cycle of parenting we looked at in Psalm 78 also mapped out for us in Deuteronomy 6. Don't you think that the fact that the Psalmist relayed a cycle that Moses initially mapped out was indicative that it was a very effective way of teaching them diligently?

Do you remember the conversation Moses modeled for us in Deuteronomy 6:20–25? It started with, "When your son asks you in time to come 'What is the meaning of the testimonies and the statutes and the rules that the LORD our God has commanded you?'" (ESV), you should tell him the following:

1. We were slaves in Egypt, and the Lord miraculously brought us out.

2. His plan was to bring us to the land He had promised to our people generations before.

3. After He brought us out of Egypt, He gave us laws, instituted celebrations to help us remember what He had done for us, and to help us live the way that pleases Him.

So, as Moses was laying the foundation for God's people to Teach Their Children Diligently, he was instructing them in exactly how to talk to their children. He wanted them to share their story with their kiddos, because through sharing the story of their past, where they had come from, and where they were going, their children were being taught great truths and given great hope that the same God at work in times past was still with them.

So, how does that correspond to talking to our children in the church age in which we all live? Pretty closely, actually. Let's take a look.

Although we teach our children about the plagues, the exodus from Egypt, the wilderness wanderings, and the eventual arrival into the Promised Land, those are not "our" stories. No. By God's amazing grace, we have an even more intimate and powerful story to tell our children. By following the template Moses laid out for us, let's see how telling our children our story can be used mightily to strengthen their faith and lead them to a heart knowledge and relationship with God — and to even having their own story to pass on to their children one day. It's pretty amazing how closely our own story was modeled for us by God's work for the children of Israel. Adding your own unique details to the overall story will allow your children to get an up-close-and-personal look at the work of God and to get to know you even better. David and I have been amazed at how powerful our testimonies have been through the years as we have discipled our children.

I doubt this will ever be handled in as formal a way as I am writing it, of course, for it is but a template of a conversation, a jumping off point for you. Notice that Moses said,

"When your son asks..." you say ". . . ." More often than not, the best conversations we have had with our children have actually started with one of their questions. As I interact with my children each day, I think often of Peter's exhortation to always be ready to give an answer whenever we're asked about the hope that is in us (1 Peter 3:15), and I am so thankful that God always gives me the words to say in answer to them when I ask Him to.

So, using Moses' template, the next time your child opens the door by asking a question about your own story, here's how your conversation could go:

1. I was in bondage to sin with no hope of breaking free on my own. I was a slave to the chains of sin with no hope of having fellowship with the God who created me. Throughout His Word, though, God tells me that He loves me and wants to be my God.

2. So, God miraculously intervened and rescued me from slavery. By laying down His perfect life for me and then rising again, He made a way for me and all who believe on His name to escape the chains that held us. We see His plan for my rescue in John 3:16 — "For God so loved the world that He gave His only begotten Son, that whosoever believeth in Him should not perish, but have everlasting life." Jesus was not willing that any should perish away from Him, but that all should come to repentance (2 Peter 3:9), so He Himself made a way for me to cross the impossible gap that kept me from God.

3. This rescue was in fulfillment of all the promises He had made throughout His Word. Jesus, God Himself in the flesh, entered our world for the purpose of saving us and teaching us how to live, and

He wants us to love and serve Him here on earth
and eventually live with Him eternally in heaven.

Pretty similar story, isn't it? And, if God was so confident in
that method of teaching the children of Israel their story of
redemption for so many centuries, don't you believe that He
will still use it in your family today?

So, the question is, have you told your children your
story? Have they been introduced to the mighty power of
God by seeing His hand at work in you? God gave David
and me very different stories. David accepted Jesus as His
Savior when he was 24 years old. By that time, he had experienced many things that were an affront to a Holy God.
I, on the other hand, came to know Jesus as a very young
child. For years, I felt like my story was much less powerful
than David's, for he was saved out of a life of alcoholism and
desperate sin. As I have watched my children grow and have
talked to them about my story, though, I have realized that
just the opposite is true. My story is of God's incredible grace
that saved me FROM a life of alcoholism and desperate sin.
It is an incredibly powerful story — and the story I have
prayed my children will be able to tell to their own children
one day.

Even though each of my children came to accept Jesus'
free gift of salvation at a young age, they still have stories
of change and exciting tales they can pass on to their own
children one day. It was evident that Payton, in particular,
had a pretty severe inner struggle going on as the Lord was
convicting him of his sinfulness and need of a Savior. He
started exhibiting bad behaviors that he knew were wrong,
and the days leading to his salvation were full of frustration
for both him and me. The change of heart and countenance
in that little boy, though, when he finally humbled his own
strong will to the will of Jesus was remarkable. I would not
have believed that one so young could display such a huge

difference in manner of life, yet he did. God's work in his life was clearly evident and provides a story for him to tell his children in the years ahead.

Telling your story isn't limited to your salvation story, though. Recounting how God has worked in your life and in your family — wonderful tales of His provision, protection, and direction — are incredible ways to share your faith and teach your children diligently.

This was something my parents did exceptionally well. Through my growing up years, I saw God high and lifted up more times than I can count. Despite all the amazing things God did for our family, the one that stands out the most in my mind as I think back was a very small thing that happened when I was too young to even know we had a need.

Mom and Dad have often told me about a time just before my younger sister's first birthday, when they didn't even have enough money to be able to have a birthday cake or any celebration for her at all. In the grand scheme of things, of course, a child's first birthday celebration isn't a massive deal, but God cared. He cared about my parents. He cared about my sister. He cared about our family, and He used that small situation to teach us all a huge lesson.

On the day of Kristin's birthday, a card came in the mail from my great uncle, and in that card was a $5 bill. Never before or after that time did that uncle send anything more than a funny card for a birthday, but God used him at that moment to strengthen the faith of my parents, show them His love, and weave a story of His grace into the tapestry of our family.

My parent's account of that simple situation and how God used it in their lives taught my young heart that God loved me. I came to understand that He loves me so much that He even cares about small things in my life, and He is powerful enough to be trusted to take care of the big things as well. Growing up in a Christian family did not necessarily strengthen my faith, but growing up in a home where my parents told the stories of God's work in their lives certainly did.

✦ ✦ ✦ ✦

So, how about you? Why don't you take a few minutes right now to thank God for your own unique story of redemption and the many things He has done in and for you and your family? Meditate on your own story and marvel in the wonder of it all. Purpose in your heart to share your stories with your children and anyone else God brings across your path as often and in as many ways as you can. If you aren't sure what I mean by your story of redemption, ask God to reveal Himself to you right now. Ask Him to show you how you, too, can be rescued from the slavery of sin. Take a moment to search "God's Plan of Salvation" to learn more about that story. Bible.org has a great article that really lays out just how helpless we are to bridge the gap between us and God.

Chapter 10

What Are We Going For?
How Do We Get There?

As I noted earlier, the Lord gave David and I some pretty amazing mentors to learn from and emulate when we were just cutting our parenting teeth. Paul Whitt, who is currently serving as an associate pastor in North Carolina, was one of those amazing mentors. To this day, he regularly shares #parentingthought posts on his Facebook page to encourage and help those of us who are still "in the trenches," so to speak. As God would have it, a Facebook Timehop reminder of his post from a year or so ago popped up just as I was praying about writing this book, and it served as a great reminder to me that we have to have a definite plan for where we want our children to end up if we are going to formulate a strategy for how to guide them there. Paul wrote:

> Parenting Thought: Prayerfully decide away from the noise what you want your children to know and love when they leave your home, and purposely and consistently model it and teach them. There will be new distractions and competition for your time as they grow older, so remain committed to those most important goals. Your days of captive influence and instruction will be over before you know it. Loving God. Loving His Word. Loving the gospel story.

Loving others, and loving the church are good places to start. #Parentingthought[1]

The goals Paul lays out there should be the very basic goals we all have for our children. They echo right back to what Moses told the children of Israel was the ultimate purpose of teaching them diligently — that they may love the Lord their God with all their heart, soul, and might — and it encompasses Jesus' addition to that great commandment that we are to love others more than we love ourselves.

As I thought about that idea and prayed even more, I realized that I had been using God's "handbook of parenting" for years without even realizing it. God's Word tells us in 2 Peter 1:3 that He has given us everything we need to know to live a life that is full and pleasing to Him. Once again, if God is a God who can be trusted, we must acknowledge that this statement also encompasses that elusive parenting manual.

Years ago, I compiled some of my notes from prayer journals and put together a prayer guide for children that we have made available through the Teach Them Diligently blog. These are verses that I have prayed regularly for my own children since they were very young, but I didn't realize until I was studying for this book that what I was praying and actively putting into practice was actually following the parenting guide God had given us in His Word. Each day as I prayed specifically for my children, sought God's face on their behalf, and studied His Word, my focus was on the things I wanted my children to know and to become. Without ever creating a checklist or even being wise enough to realize what we were doing, the way David and I were parenting our children was being directed by God's very clear, very inclusive parenting manual. Our goals for our children, the way we were praying, the traits and priorities we wanted for them that were on the forefront of our minds were the exact things God wants all His children to know and learn. David and I were learning and growing and passing what we learned on to our children each day . . . teaching them diligently, humbly, and naturally!

So, what do we find in God's manual? A LOT! Without time or space in this volume to write all that we find, allow me to give you a taste of the parenting instructions we find in God's Word. I hope they will whet your own appetite to search the Bible for even more and to incorporate all these into your own lives and then impart them to your children as you, too, teach them diligently.

Let's look at a just few of the passages that I have been praying and encouraging others to pray for their children for years and see just how a focus on those things can affect our parenting styles, decisions, and more. You'll see in each one that, even as we are seeking to mold our children into the image of God, God will also be working in our own lives, making us more fit for service as well. What a great God we serve, and what an amazing plan for His families He has laid out.

May they know the Scriptures, which are able to make them wise unto salvation. "And that from a child thou hast known the holy scriptures, which are able to make thee wise unto salvation through faith which is in Christ Jesus" (2 Timothy 3:15).

For most of us, the prayer of our hearts is that each of our children will come to know the Lord as their personal Savior at a very young age. By focusing on this prayer, we are much more tuned in to situations where natural conversation about the truths of Scripture opens doors for us to lay the foundation for their future faith. We also become much more focused on making sure we are introducing them to the Scriptures every chance we get. What this prayer does for us as parents is make us dig deeper into Scripture, so we are able to shepherd their hearts even better.

As I noted earlier, most of our days for many years has started with all of us sitting around the table talking about what God is teaching us in our own personal devotions. Those conversations help to hold me accountable for being in God's Word each day looking for the truths He has for me and what He has for me to share with my children, so they, too, will get a deep hunger and thirst for Him at a young age. Now that they're older, it is exciting to hear them draw personal applications from the passages they are reading.

May they grow in the grace and knowledge of Jesus Christ. "But grow in grace, and in the knowledge of our Lord and Saviour Jesus Christ. To him be glory both now and for ever. Amen" (2 Peter 3:18).

If my focus is on them growing in the grace and knowledge of our Lord and Savior Jesus Christ, I will be looking for every opportunity to present Him to them, to share His works and His ways with them, to help them see how practical His directives actually are and how trustworthy are His words. With this on my mind each day, I find that I see His hand more clearly at work and the wisdom of His plan more clearly manifested through each situation, because I am looking for Him. I have grown in grace and knowledge in countless ways through praying this prayer for my children, and they have a natural inclination to look for God at work because of the focus that has always been in our home.

May they say no to sin. "My son, if sinners entice thee, consent thou not" (Proverbs 1:10).

We live in a culture that frowns on calling sin by its name. We are confronted on every side by political correctness, watered-down theology, and more. Satan has caused us as parents to live in fear of creating "bullies" or "unloving people" if we talk to them very directly about sin. Yet, without a clear view of sin, the wages of it won't matter as much.

David and I have spent a lot of time talking to our children about why God hates sin — He is holy and wants us to be holy as well. We've discussed with them why they should avoid sin at all costs by explaining the ramifications of the choices they make, how sin always costs more than they want to pay, and so on. Now that they're older and being confronted with way more temptation and seeing people very close to them making choices that may well scar them for life, they have come to hate sin as well, for it has profound effects on people they love.

If each of us, as their parents, though, don't have a right view of sin, it will be impossible to pass one on to our children. This echoes back to keeping God's commandments and being obedient. If we make allowances for things that God says are an abomination, we will have a very hard time instilling in our children a heart that flees temptation and runs from situations where they may fall into sin. Oh, that God will give His people a heart that hates sin and runs from it, even as we show His love to those who are caught in its snare. For compassion on sinners is also a great way that God uses parents to point their children to Him, as we will see in a bit.

May they be quick to forgive. "And be ye kind one to another, tenderhearted, forgiving one another, even as God for Christ's sake hath forgiven you" (Ephesians 4:32).

This is a very easy one to start teaching to your children at a very young age. Being kind and forgiving is always first learned in our homes. It can then prove to be a powerful lesson that will serve them well throughout their lives. A focus on kindness and forgiving siblings — and even parents who are humble enough to ask forgiveness of their children for their own failures — is teaching and modeling a life that loves God and others wholeheartedly.

As parents, we need to model kindness and forgiveness as well. I have struggled from time to time with this, and God has convicted me greatly. Through the years, there have been situations where something has been done to or said about our family that has been incredibly hurtful. Satan has tried hard to use those things to make my heart hard or bitter. There have been times when my words have been biting. Just a few weeks ago, I allowed a harsh statement to leave my lips.

My oldest, in incredibly wise fashion, looked at me and said kindly, "You're pretty hard on them." That rebuke was well-placed. I *was* being pretty hard on them. Immediately, I asked God to forgive me, and within minutes, I thanked Camden for calling me out on that, and I apologized to him for the attitude I was showing. He was displaying a heart that was far more kind and forgiving than mine was at that moment, and God graciously used him to help his mama get her heart right.

May they choose the right friends. "He that walketh with wise men shall be wise: but a companion of fools shall be destroyed" (Proverbs 13:20).

Do you know your children's friends? Do you talk to them about those they hang out with? Do you coach them in their relationships? We have purposely set up our home to be the place where our children and their friends want to hang out. We have inherited several extra "sons and daughters" in the process, and we know our teens' friends very well. Our children know that their friends are always welcome in our home and that we genuinely love them, so when we see things in their friends' lives that concern us, we have a very natural platform to talk to them about it.

We have taught our children that the ones they hang out with says much about what's in their heart, and we have seen them choose friends who, generally speaking, have a heart for the Lord. We have seen our children take stands with their friends and truly be used to sharpen others through their walk and through their words. What a joy this has been.

As parents, please get to know your children's friends. Not only will it be a blessing to you to be part of your children's lives that way, but you will also find that it gives you great insight into what others may be struggling with and what your children are facing each day. Find ways to join in their activities when possible. In our home, David and I play a lot of volleyball and basketball with our children and their friends, for that is what they like to do. It's fun. It's a natural way to build relationships, and quite frankly, it keeps us in shape and feeling a little younger than we actually are. Getting to know your children's friends will also open opportunities that you would have never imagined to minister to other young people. I can't tell you how often I have heard David having long, deep conversations with several teen boys around our table — simply because they trust him and like to talk to him.

May they have no ungodly strongholds. "For though we walk in the flesh, we do not war after the flesh: (For the weapons of our warfare are not carnal, but mighty through God to the pulling down of strong holds)" (2 Corinthians 10:3–4).

The older I get, the more clearly I see that the battle raging all around us is truly spiritual in nature. Far too often, I see young and old alike enslaved to sins that they simply cannot seem to break free from. How I pray that God will keep my children from ever allowing those strongholds of sin to take root in their lives.

Sometimes, guarding against strongholds means having difficult conversations with your children. Sometimes, it means digging in your heels and not allowing them to cross lines that you know could be deadly in the long run. Sometimes it means setting boundaries in place that protect them from being exposed to things that can become addictive or enslaving.

This element of our parenting is one of the hardest, for it is not always as natural. I don't like feeling that I'm nagging my children or keeping them from doing what they believe will bring them happiness. But, I'm willing to do it, for I know what can happen if their judgment becomes impaired, and they put themselves in a position for Satan to take control of an area of their lives or mind.

This is also an area of parenting where Satan can use fear to enslave you as the mom or dad. I know, for he has done it to me. He has made me become so aware of the dangers all around my children, that I had a hard time trusting God to protect them. I ran the risk of allowing that fear to become a stronghold in my own life. Once again, I was able to see how God will use my prayerful focus on Him on behalf of my children to increase my own faith. He convicted me of my sin and made me aware of what the tempter was trying to do. I grew in my own walk with God through praying this prayer for my children, for I learned that, though I need to be vigilantly watching and guarding my kiddos, ultimately God could be trusted for their protection.

There is not room here to go through all 36 of the prayers that I have in the prayer guide, let alone the countless others we find in Scripture, but I wanted to highlight a few to show how using Scripture to set your parenting course and your goals for your children will not only give you direction and focus each day, but it will also help you to grow as a Christian even as you watch your children grow.

What a masterful plan God laid out for families!

❖ ❖ ❖ ❖

Have you taken time to prayerfully consider what you want your children to know and love by the time they are ready to leave your home? Does what you know and love line up with those goals? Do you have a strategy in place for making sure you use every opportunity you are given to point your children in the direction of what you know God has for them? I invite you to stop for a little while and pray that God shows you from His Word what you should be expecting from your children. Go to the Teach Them Diligently blog and download the prayer guide for children to help direct your thoughts on this matter even more. I hope you will start to notice how God will grow and change you in amazing ways as you teach your children diligently.

Endnotes

1. https://www.facebook.com/paul.whitt.

Chapter 11

Sometimes "Teach Them Diligently" Gets Very Personal

Mama, did you know that Noah's ark was not cute like it is on church nursery walls?"

That completely random statement came from my 10-year-old while we were driving to pick up her big sister from volleyball practice one afternoon.

She went on. "It was really scary to people! We watched a short video that showed what the earth may have looked like as the Flood came, and it must have been horrifying."

Not feeling that it was the best time to remind her that we had discussed that very fact and even watched that video together, I decided to capitalize on the discipleship moment that was started during her geography class at our homeschool co-op earlier that day.

"I know!" I replied. "Can you imagine how scary it must have been to see the waters coming at you like that? What was the only way those people could have been safe?"

"They had to be in the ark to be safe."

"That's right. Only those in the ark were safe, but they were completely protected from the danger that was outside, weren't they? Did you ever think that the ark may even help us remember something even bigger? What is the only way for us who are alive right now to be truly safe for always?"

"To be in Jesus."

"Exactly, Jesus offered us safety for all eternity, didn't He? He told us that whoever the Father puts in His hand, no one is able to pluck them out. Pretty amazing, huh?"

As we continued talking in the car, that exchange turned very personal for me. God impressed on my heart just how often I forget that I am safe; how often I allow the dangers all around me to distract and even paralyze me; and how much I need to be reminded, just like I was reminding my daughter, that no matter what big waves I see coming toward me, God will never let me go.

Lila and I turned on a recording of Keith and Kristyn Getty's "He Will Hold Me Fast," and sang along for the rest of the ride to the gym, but the Lord kept reminding me of those truths well beyond that short car ride. I am safe in Him. I can rely on Him. I can run to Him. He WILL hold me fast.

Praise the Lord that He often uses those discipleship moments we spend with our children to grow our own faith as well. For not only do we as Christian parents find our faith strengthened as we are discipling our children, but very often, God uses our role as parent to deeply refine us as individuals.

I was talking to a group of ladies recently, and at one point in our conversation, it was noted how often our children struggle with very similar things that we do. Shortly thereafter, a young mom at our church shared a story with me and gave me permission to share it with you, for it shows just how much God can use your children, no matter how young they are, to illuminate attitudes and actions that need to be removed from your life.

Here is what I have been learning through discipleship this week. My oldest daughter, who is three, has been regressing in a lot of ways recently. Things we thought we had mastered have gone by the wayside, and old, ugly behaviors have crept back in. When she gets mad or frustrated, she screams, she kicks, or she hits things. About six months ago, we had her memorize the fruits of the Spirit verses. Whenever an ugly behavior would present itself, we would sit down for a chat. I would ask her, "Was that behavior loving . . . joyful . . . peaceful . . . patient . . . etc.? Did you have your self-control?" Usually the answer was "no" to all the above. We would then talk through ways that she could have done it differently and have a do-over. She gets to try the situation again using those fruits of the Spirit. Though there are consequences for her actions, and she always has to apologize, we hug it out, and I praise her for the right reactions she shows on her re-do. Sometimes we go through that same exercise many times a day, with me always wondering if she's even listening.

Not long ago, I remembered the verse in Ephesians 4, where we are told to "Be angry, and sin not" [verse 26]. I can't believe it took me almost four years to remember to tell her that it's okay to be mad, but she has to learn that her response cannot be sinful but has to represent all the fruits we have been talking about.

Yesterday, I had a very short rope. She disobeyed about something that was pretty insignificant in hindsight, but I lost it. I yelled at her. I used unkind words. I got angry. She was crying, and I was crying. I knew I had to swallow my words and do the hard work of apologizing. I often try to downplay it and convince myself that she needed to hear that. Maybe she did need to hear some of it, but I'm learning that two wrongs don't make a right.

When my husband got home, I left the girls with him and went into my daughter's room and just sat on her bed to cry. And I prayed. Lots of crying and lots of praying. In just a little while, she came in and sat on my lap, and we cried together for almost ten minutes. Then I said my apology. I reassured her that I love her, and that I was wrong for being angry that way. I was wrong for not using my words for kindness or with patience. I said I was wrong, and I asked her to forgive me.

She sat up, stopped crying, and lovingly put her hand on my shoulder, and in her oh-so-mature-three-year-old voice, repeated what she had heard me say to her many times, "Oh, Mommy! It's going to be okay! Sometimes you get mad, and that's okay. Did you know that the Bible says it's okay to be mad? We just need to work on your response because that verse says be mad and don't sin."

Crickets. . . .

She does listen! She hears me in spite of all my imperfections as a parent. God still uses terrible yelling moments to grow our relationship into one of open communication. It was so freeing to be forgiven by a three-year-old. It was almost as if God needed to level the playing field and remind me that I am just as much a sinner as she is, even though I am older and "wiser." We all make mistakes. We all need forgiveness.

From the mouths of babes.

Oh, how I saw myself through that young mom's story. There have been so many times that God has used my children and my own failures to teach us both lessons about walking with Him. Never allow Satan to get away with whispering to you that you are not worthy of such a high calling as parenting or that you could never consistently point your children to Christ and model His love for them. That is simply not true. God created you specifically to be the parent of those He put into your home. He created them to be uniquely designed to learn from you. He gave you the incredible privilege and platform to shape their little hearts and minds and give them a hunger and thirst for the things of the Lord. And He wants all of you to be growing more like Him together. How amazing is that?

When I was growing up, if you would have asked me if my parents knew what they were doing, I would have answered with a resounding "Yes." Even as a youngster, I stood in awe of their wisdom and balance. I appreciated their humility and the way they always told me the "whys" behind what they believed.

What I didn't know then that I know now is how much they were growing even as they were teaching me. Neither of them came to know the Lord when they were very young like I did. Neither of them went to Christian school or got to attend AWANA and learn tons of Scripture like I did. Neither of them had any formal Bible training, yet they were actively learning more about God and His ways even as they were teaching my sister and me every single day.

They told us stories of God's grace. They engaged us in conversations about what we were learning or how we were growing. They modeled for us Christ-like character, hospitality, love, and forgiveness. We grew to become great friends and brothers and sisters in Christ as Kristin and I got older.

My mom and dad were not anyone of note to most of the world, but they were the perfect vessels for God to use to instill in us a deep love for God and His Word, and now they are enjoying the benefits of watching their children follow in their footsteps and teach their six grandchildren diligently to walk in His ways.

I am sure that if I could go back in time and ask my parents how they thought they were doing as parents when we were growing up, they, too, would have felt unworthy and unable. But God showed that He was able to not only cause them to grow in their faith, but to also increase faith in Kristin and me at the same time.

✦ ✦ ✦ ✦

Do you ever feel like you are unable or unworthy to be a parent? Has Satan tried to convince you that you are destined to fail in this pursuit? Oh, my dear friend, turn your eyes upon Jesus! Recognize that in your weakness, He is made strong. Ask Him to help you and your children become more like Him together. Ask Him to show both of you the areas of your life that you need to turn over to Him to become conformed to His image.

Chapter 12

How Can We Tell It's Working?

I'm a homeschool mom, and as such, I often do evaluations with my children. I want to know if they are getting their work done, if they are truly learning the material, if they are progressing in such a way that I can tell they will be prepared for the next stage of their lives, and so on.

The older they have gotten, I have noticed that my evaluations have shifted a bit. I am less focused on their actual work, although that's still a very important tool for me, for I have become more focused on the character, work ethic, tender heart, etc. that is indicative of one who is mature. By God's grace, I'm starting to see my children walking in such a way that they, too, will be poised to teach diligently in the days ahead.

As we have noted throughout these pages, we see that Scripture is sufficient to tell us where we're headed and to show us how we know teaching them diligently is accomplishing what we hoped it would. The Apostle Paul gave us an example of the traits and outcomes we should be looking for in our own children's lives through his instruction to his child in the Lord, Timothy. He even gave us a good "rubric" on which to evaluate the growth of our children.

Paul met Timothy when Timothy was quite young. We are told that his mom was Jewish and his father was Greek. We are also told that God used the faith of his mother Eunice and his grandmother Lois to instill in Timothy a faith in Jesus as well. Though his background wasn't ideal, since he had an unbelieving father, God still used the discipleship efforts of the women in his life to prepare Timothy for the work He had for him.

Timothy was a regular companion of Paul's, and we see that he was well-thought-of by Paul and other believers of his day. Throughout many of Paul's letters, we see the Apostle's discipleship of his "son." First Timothy gives us a great glimpse into the instruction Paul had for Timothy as a pastor, and I strongly encourage you to dive in as you are constructing your own copy of the biblical "parenting manual," for there is much for us to learn there. In that letter, Paul tells Timothy that "the end of the commandment [the goal, the finish, what Paul was trying to get Timothy to shoot for] is charity out of a pure heart, and of a good conscience, and of faith unfeigned" (1 Timothy 1:5). Paul tells Timothy that the goal of all his teaching was that Timothy love God and people with a heart that is pure, a conscience that is unstained, and a faith that is sincere and strong. That's quite a parental mission statement, isn't it?

As Paul was preparing to pass off the scene, he reached out to Timothy one last time in the letter of 2 Timothy. He seems to have been concerned that Timothy's faith might be shaken. Perhaps he was feeling the weight of his own suffering, and concerned that Satan would use that to draw Timothy away from the Lord. Perhaps there were things going on in Timothy's life or within his church that Paul feared would affect his walk with God. Whatever the cause, we see Paul acting very much like a parent concerned for his child in the way he approaches his younger friend.

We hear Paul telling Timothy to stir up his gift, replace fear with love, power, and a sound mind, and not to be ashamed of Paul or of the gospel. Rather, Timothy was instructed to willingly suffer for the gospel and hold on to the truth. Later in the letter, Timothy is told to be strong, to put his confidence in the Scriptures, and to preach it continuously.

Throughout the letter, Paul gives us an idea of what to look for in order to know that our discipleship efforts are being blessed, and that our children are being sharpened to the point that they are becoming fit for the Master's service.

They will hold fast to the teaching they have been given (2 Timothy 1:13).

As our children get older, they start making more and more decisions on their own. They form their own belief system. They become the man or woman it is in their heart to become. So, we should be watching for signs that they are holding fast to what we have taught them. What is in their heart will always spill out and become visible. Paul reminds Timothy that he has a sacred stewardship of the good thing that was given to him, and he is responsible for continuing to walk in it.

What a joy Timothy must have been to Paul, for he certainly held fast to the teaching the Apostle had given him. He walked with God, carried on Paul's work, and was used mightily. No wonder Paul could write of his pleasure in seeing Timothy and others live their faith. That was a clear sign that God had done a mighty work in their lives. Isn't it amazing that by His grace, He most often uses the influence of godly parents to accomplish that?

They will stand strong (2 Timothy 2).

Paul gives Timothy the exact same exhortation King David gave Solomon as he was about to die. Be strong and show yourself a man (1 Kings 2:2). These dads had spent their lives teaching their sons God's ways, His commandments, and His statutes, and modeling God's heart for them. Now it was time for them to step up, stand strong, and continue the cycle. Timothy and Solomon were instructed in how they should continue to walk in truth with their whole heart, just as David and Paul had learned years before. In both cases, we see the fathers expecting their sons to carry on the work God had started through them, and in both cases, God's plan prevails.

They will endeavor to please God (2 Timothy 2:15).

Timothy is reminded to diligently work to present himself as a genuine believer before God. The word he uses that is translated "approved" presented an incredibly practical illustration in Paul's day. You see, in that time, they didn't have a banking system akin to what we have now, nor did they have paper money. Instead, they would take the metals they used in their coins and pour them into molds to make the currency of trade. Once that molded metal cooled, it had to be shaved to make it usable, and many dishonest men would shave it so closely that it removed far too much of the metal. The honorable money changers would only put the coins into circulation which were genuine and of full weight. Thus, those men became known as *dokimos* or "approved."

What Paul was telling Timothy was not to cut corners and shave off pieces of his training to try to make his life easier. No. He was to show himself to be genuine, fully valuable, and approved unto God. He was further exhorted to rightly divide the Word of Truth. Since we know that "teach them diligently" literally means to sharpen our children to make them fit to serve the King, it should come as no surprise that what Paul is literally telling Timothy here is to cut the Word of Truth straight, making sure that when it is cut open and laid out for deeper exploration and sharing with others, it can always be put back together without a gap. There should be no adding to it or taking away from it as we present it to others. Instead, it must be handled with care and with reverence. It's interesting to note that the word Paul uses here only occurs this one time in the entire New Testament. Isn't it curious that it's in a book full of practical lessons for those of us seeking to "teach our children diligently"?

They will make choices that show that they want to be used by God (2 Timothy 2:20–26).

Next, Paul talks to Timothy about different ways he can live out his faith, how he can show others whose he is by the way he lives his life. Just as we have told our children through the years, you can tell what is in one's heart by their actions and the choices they make. So, we can have a good gauge of our children's heart for the Lord by the way they choose to live their lives.

Paul tells Timothy how he can become a vessel of high value, made holy and useful for the Master, and prepared for every good work. Isn't that what we want to see in our children? Isn't our whole purpose in teaching them diligently to sharpen them to the point that they are fully prepared to be shot out to serve God on their own and make other disciples just as Jesus commanded?

"Flee also youthful lusts: but follow righteousness, faith, charity, peace . . ." (2 Timothy 2:22). Paul reminds Timothy that the more he follows what is good, the easier it becomes to flee that which is at war within him. When we see our children making the outward decisions to walk in righteousness, faith, love, and peace, the more we will have confidence that they are winning the inner battles that we cannot see.

Avoid getting involved in foolish debates that only cause strife, but be gentle, patient, meek, and eager to teach others that they, too, may know the joy that comes through knowing God. How often the enemy uses distractions and arguments to render God's people weak or even useless. When our children learn to steer clear of those useless arguments that can destroy their credibility on matters that are important, we'll see God's hand at work in their lives. Our children are high value targets for the enemy. They must stay sharp, focused, and diligent as they learn to follow God. As their parents, we have the privilege to guide them in those ways.

They will continue in what they have learned and seen in us (2 Timothy 3).

After laying out a long list of the evils Timothy could expect to encounter, Paul reminds Timothy in verse 10 that he knows his doctrine. He has seen Paul live the truth out in front of him, modeling a life filled with purpose, patience, faith, love, and longsuffering. Timothy must now continue in what he's learned. That is the logical next step. It has been imprinted on him through years of sharpening and example.

Timothy was accustomed to these things. He had become firmly persuaded that they were true because he had years of having these truths presented to him as he walked, ate, worked, etc. He knew that Paul, too, was genuine in his faith, so he was trustworthy in his presentation of the things of the Lord. Timothy had been taught diligently, and now he was to keep going, keep growing, and keep learning from the Scriptures that he "may be perfect, thoroughly furnished unto all good works" (2 Timothy 3:17).

As our children grow and start leaving the home, our discipleship of them does not end. Quite the contrary! We have laid the foundation for them to build on, but they will still need to be mentored by their parents and other godly influences to help them as they continue on their way. How our hearts will rejoice, though, as we watch them continuing in truth and becoming more and more prepared to be the world changers we have prayed for so long that God would make them to be.

They will start to Teach Them Diligently (2 Timothy 4).

"Preach the word; be instant in season, out of season; reprove, rebuke, exhort with all long suffering and doctrine" (2 Timothy 4:2). Through his teaching and discipleship, Paul now sees his "son" ready to take up the mantle and teach others diligently. He charges him to be a herald of the good news. Tell everyone who will listen — all the time! When it's hard and when it's easy; when you want to and when you don't — teach them all diligently!

Ultimately, we will know that our discipleship efforts are working when we look at our children and know they are now ready to go out and make disciples of their own. The Great Commission will take root in them, and they will be fully prepared to parent and lead others on their own.

These evidences of our discipleship efforts having their desired effect show up in various ways throughout our children's lives. You'll notice that even the way Paul approaches them seems to show a progressive maturity. We first see them making their own the things that they have been taught. They build habits like having their devotions, talking about things of the Lord, and listening to godly music that are indicative that they are holding fast to the teaching they have been given.

Next, we'll see them start standing strong. In our culture, our children are called upon to draw lines in the sand even earlier than we were growing up. When we start seeing our children stand strong rather than give in to the temptations and peer pressure around them, we will know God is at work. Endeavoring to please God and making choices that ensure they will be usable to God go hand in hand, and we start to see those things developing in them as they start enjoying more freedoms in their teen years. At that point, our children will start seeking God on their own and ordering their lives His way. What they allow into their hearts and lives and what they don't at this point will give us insight into what they actually love, and how devoted they are to what they have learned from us. It is once they leave our nest that we actually see them continuing in what they've learned. By then, we have had plenty of opportunities as we are watching these other proofs develop or not develop in them to intervene when necessary. By praying for them and talking with them each step of the way, we will, by God's grace, see them growing in grace and continuing in what they've learned even as they head out on their own to college or whatever God has ordained for the next step of their lives.

Finally, we all long for the day when we will see our own children pouring into others what they have learned from us. How humbling of an experience to know that God used YOU, the parent of that child, to prepare him or her to serve Him. God chose YOU through the influence you had on that child to reach so many others. I can think of no greater blessing or more hopeful promise than that.

As I was writing this chapter, I pretty much had revival in my chair. When I think of how faithful God is to keep His promises, when I consider the great work He has done in my life and in the lives of my children, my heart can hardly contain its praise. I am certainly no prophet, and I cannot see into the future, but I do believe the promises that God has given me throughout His Word. I do believe He is faithful to fulfill those promises, and I do believe He will keep my children walking close to Him all the days of their lives. I had never stopped to consider the "proofs" the Lord taught me in this study, but as I evaluate them, I am humbled to say that I can see them in the lives of my children. How I pray you will see them in yours!

✤ ✤ ✤ ✤

Whatever stage of parenting you are in, whether you have little ones who have not yet grown old enough to fully understand God's love for them, or whether you have bigger ones who are starting to bear fruit on their own, I hope you will stop and thank God right now once again for the privilege of being their parent. Lay out before Him your hopes and dreams for them, and watch with anticipation for these evidences of their devotion to start appearing in their lives. I promise that when they do, you'll have the same glorious reaction I have had today.

Chapter 13

What does Discipleship-Focused Parenting NOT Look Like?

By now there should be no doubt that God has given us a plethora of instructions and principles upon which to base our parenting decisions. What we have not yet looked at, though, are the things that are not attuned to a teach-them-diligently style of parenting, things that actually break relationships instead of strengthening them. Just as the Bible gives us plenty of instruction on what discipleship-focused parenting looks like, even so we see barriers to the natural relationships that you would expect to see in a godly parent-child relationship. If we are walking in the fear of God, keeping God's commandments and statutes, and growing in grace even as we teach our children diligently, the traits and actions that God warns us against should not be definitive of our lives as parents.

It's likely that the first parenting negative that popped into your mind is Paul's exhortation to parents in Colossians 3:21: "Provoke not your children to anger, lest they be discouraged." Though addressed to fathers, this command is generally understood to apply to us moms as well, and is literally telling us not to anger or exasperate our children. This refers to a habitual pattern of behavior from a parent that will cause resentment and discouragement to build up to the point that it causes a great rift in their relationship with their children.

It certainly gives us much to talk about as we examine what discipleship-focused parenting does not look like. There are a myriad of ways we as parents can provoke our children to wrath, and they are not all because we are angry or harsh ourselves. Since there is no way to effectively teach our children diligently if our relationship with them is strained, we must make sure that the way we approach and interact with our children is not starting a cycle that could lead to a break. Let's examine just a few ways parents can provoke their children to wrath, and what can be done to correct it.

Creating an environment where they believe they are doing right simply for the sake of appearances can provoke our children to wrath. There is not enough space in this book to share the stories of people I know who have completely walked away from their faith because they were never passed on "faith" to begin with. Rather, they were told what to do and what not to do with high expectations set on things everyone could see instead of a deep focus being put on what was growing in their hearts. Setting expectations on actions sets them up for failure, for only God can create a heart that wants to keep His commandments and statutes. This superficial works-based religion has led many to become bitter and completely deaf to the words of the gospel. A teach-them-diligently style of parenting never focuses simply on the visible actions of their children, but goes way down to the root of those actions instead. As has been noted before, we must focus on getting to the heart of the matter; for out of their heart, their words and actions will spring.

Raising our children by fear instead of faith is another way we can set up an environment that is so restrictive that it can lead to a break in your relationship. As parents, we are certainly called upon to protect our children as much as we can and to create an environment for them that is safe and will help them grow in their faith. As they get older, though, there are usually some boundaries that you can move a bit to allow them to stretch their own "faith muscles" and put it into practice in a controlled environment. Our oldest has always gained additional freedoms before our youngest. As we have been growing together, I have seen him mature, and I believe that he can be trusted to make wise decisions. Therefore, I can allow him to spread his wings a bit more than I did even a year ago. When I have allowed my fear of losing him, of him making a bad decision, or of him getting hurt to guide my decisions, and I have not given him the freedoms he is mature enough to handle, I have seen the hurt in his eyes. I came to realize that the hurt is not an anger at being told no, but rather the realization that he has not earned my trust.

If after repeated attempts to earn our trust, our children are never given it, they will assume they can't win it. They will be provoked, and they will be more likely to rebel than if we had given them a taste of freedom with the "training wheels" still attached to allow us to continue to guide them through this next step of growing up. Fearful parenting manifests itself in different ways at different times of our children's lives, but in each stage we are creating a world for them that is not based in reality. When our children get their first taste of reality — a world with consequences, a world that comes with hurts or failures — they may feel betrayed and unprepared to face it. We have the opportunity to shepherd our children's hearts through hurts and failures when they are in our homes, and we need to spend the time to do so. Sheltering them from pain or consequences only sets them up for a long struggle into adulthood and can cause great frustration and discouragement for them at a time when they are trying to become the man or woman God created them to be.

Our children are incredibly insightful, and they don't miss a thing. So, if you are one person at church and another at home, they will notice. As we discussed earlier, we parents are commanded to walk in the fear of the Lord and to obey

His commandments. We cannot expect our children to "do as I say and not as I do," or we are certain to provoke them to wrath. The Bible commands our children to honor their parents, and in a family where relationships are strong and faith is authentic, that should never be an issue for them. If we are modeling for them a hypocritical religion, we cannot expect them to honor us, and it's likely they will become bitter or discouraged in their own faith.

Making our children fear us is another way we parents can break the natural relationship we have with them. The Bible tells us "There is no fear in love; but perfect love casteth out fear: because fear hath torment" (1 John 4:18). The news is full of stories of battered or abused children. Even in our churches, there are children who are scared to death of their parents, and this should never be. As parents, we must exercise self-control in our words and actions, whether we are disciplining our children or just having a bad day. Proverbs 12:18 tells us that our rash words are like thrusting a sword into our child's heart. Allowing our passions to run unchecked and taking our frustrations or anger out on our children in any way will lead to a break in your relationship with them. Anytime you do overreact, or speak or act harshly to them, please ask God to forgive you and change you, and immediately ask them for their forgiveness as well.

Sometimes we parents forget that God has not called us to be everywhere, He has called us to be somewhere. We can get so concerned about getting involved in other people's lives — whether physically or virtually — that we are not nearly as involved as we should be in the lives of those who should be most dear to us. Too many children have been sacrificed on the altar of ministry to others, or a career, or simply selfish pursuits. We cannot get involved in our children's lives only when problems arise or when they have done something that embarrasses us, prompting us to "lower the boom" on them. No. That will most certainly provoke them to wrath and further break your already tenuous relationship. A teach-them-diligently parent works around the clock to build a relationship with that child, so when he does stumble, we have a much better idea what's going on below the surface and a much better footing on which to start those hard conversations.

❖ ❖ ❖ ❖

There is no way to give a complete list of what discipleship-focused parenting doesn't look like, but these are some of the ways that we often see within our churches. May we all search God's Word with an open heart, asking Him to convict us whenever we allow something to enter our lives that could break our relationship with our children and eventually provoke them to wrath. The Bible tells us much about the power of our words, about anger, about showing partiality, and about walking in the spirit. I encourage you to do a topical study on any areas that may be a weakness for you to see how God instructs you to conquer it. James 1:5 tells us, "If any of you lack wisdom, let him ask of God, that giveth to all men liberally, and upbraideth not; and it shall be given him." What a joy to know that God promises to give us wisdom anytime we seek His face and ask Him for it. He will show us how to overcome the issues that threaten our relationship with our children, and He will give us the wisdom to parent them His way.

Chapter 14

Raising Children of Promise

Oh, friends! By now I hope that you see that parenting children God's way is not at all left to chance or a cause for confusion, nor is it reason to fear. Rather, discipleship-focused, teach-them-diligently parenting is the most hopeful endeavor we will ever embark upon, and we can embark upon it in total confidence that God is faithful and able to do that which He promised. We can have great peace each day of our lives. By doing things God's way in our parenting, we will see Him not only change us from the inside out, but also He will do a mighty work in the hearts and lives of our children. He wants to use us to set up a heritage of godly families that will follow us for generations to come, impacting countless lives.

We have seen that our relationships are the key to raising children of promise. Starting with our own relationship with our loving Heavenly Father, and then building on that to create deep, meaningful relationships with our children, we have explored how God has given us everything we need to know how to parent our children His way.

At the very beginning of recorded time, God made man in His own image. He then made woman out of man and told them to go become parents (Genesis 1). At the end of creation, God called all He had made "good." All was right. All was working just as God had created it to work.

It wasn't long, though, until mankind fell for the deception of the serpent, and sin entered the world. That changed everything and set the family up as a primary battleground between God and Satan, for Satan became aware that God's plan for the family was big.

Since the family is so important to God, it's not surprising that He gives us so many promises to cling to as we build and nurture our families. Before we conclude, let's take a look at some of the outcomes the Bible says we should be looking for, always remembering how faithful God is to keep that which He has promised.

We see in Proverbs 31 that a mom (and I'm sure the same can be said of dads!) who fears the Lord and walks in His ways will be highly respected both by her children and those who know her. Proverbs 31:28 tells us "Her children arise up, and call her blessed; her husband also, and he praiseth her." Although I can't speak for you, I can say that from my perspective there can be no higher praise. Having my children and my husband respect me and value me is about as good as it gets here on earth.

Great joy is also promised to those who parent their children God's way. Proverbs 23:24–26 says, "The father of the righteous shall greatly rejoice: and he that begetteth a wise child shall have joy of him. Thy father and thy mother shall be glad, and she that bare thee shall rejoice. My son, give me thine heart, and let thine eyes observe my ways." Do your children know the joy their Christ-likeness brings to you? Are you asking them daily to give you their heart, even if you don't actually phrase it that way? As my children grow older, and I get a glimpse of what it looks like to see them walking in truth on their own, I am thankful to be able to truly understand this joy.

We have rest when our children walk with God. Raising children of promise is not for the faint of heart or for the lazy. It's natural, but it still takes diligent effort and laser focus.

We have to be consistent and active the entire time they are with us. It is certainly tiring sometimes. So, how awesome is it that God promises in Proverbs 29:17, "Correct thy son, and he shall give thee rest; yea, he shall give delight unto thy soul"? I have not yet reached the rest time since I still have four children in my home. We are deeply entrenched in the correction stage, but oh, the rest and delight that is promised when I finish this leg of my race, and I can stand in awe of the men and women of promise God has created through our family!

There are many great tangible and spiritual blessings promised to families who walk in God's ways. Psalm 112 gives us great hope for the man who fears the Lord as it recounts many blessings that are to come for him. The first blessing the Psalmist notes, though, is that our children for generations will be strong and blessed upon the earth. We find a promise for deliverance for our children in Proverbs 11:21, and Isaiah 65 tells us of a day that is coming when all those who live righteously will experience a new heaven and a new earth, with blessings and reasons to rejoice that are beyond our wildest dreams. Oh, the joys of serving Jesus and raising our children His way!

The very last words of the Old Testament point us right back to the law of Moses, because looking back and learning from what has taken place is always critical for future success. Malachi tells us:

> Remember ye the law of Moses my servant, which I commanded unto him in Horeb for all Israel, with the statutes and judgments. Behold, I will send you Elijah the prophet before the coming of the great and dreadful day of the LORD: And he shall turn the heart of the fathers to the children, and the heart of the children to their fathers, lest I come and smite the earth with a curse (Malachi 4:4–6).

There is indeed a great day of victory coming for those who love the Lord. God's plan for mankind is not yet finished, and what we are doing to prepare for that great day of the Lord is not menial. God, in His infinite wisdom, reminds us of that through a clear and pointed reference to parents. The work we are doing day in and day out, teaching our children diligently, strengthening our relationships with them, and raising children of promise is preparing them and those God brings across their paths for that promised day when His work on earth will indeed be done. There is no greater work than that.

✤ ✤ ✤ ✤

As I was studying to write this book, I came across an old song I had never sung before, but it encapsulates in verse much of what God has been teaching me, so I wanted to mention it to you before we conclude. Barbara B. Hart wrote the lyrics for "A Christian Home" in the mid-20th century, and they have been sung to the same tune as "Be Still My Soul." The song speaks of families built on faith who live out this faith daily, no matter the circumstances. May this be our prayer as we each build "A Christian Home" of our own.

Chapter 15

A List of Practical Ideas for Discipleship

Before we conclude, I wanted to share with you a list of some great discipleship ideas, thoughts, and resources from our family or that have been shared with me by Teach Them Diligently Convention families and friends. I hope these ideas will spark even more ideas of your own as you seek to utilize every opportunity God affords you to Teach Your Children Diligently, so you can raise children of promise.

- Intentional mealtime conversation that is directed at learning the hearts of your children. Of course, that takes for granted that you are making time to have meals together as often as possible. If you find conversation difficult or unnatural to get flowing at your table, perhaps you and your spouse could brainstorm some conversation starters to get your family used to deeper conversations. This is not to say that every conversation at your table needs to be discipleship-oriented and serious. Quite the contrary. In our family, the majority of our conversations are completely laughable. We giggle and play a lot together, but at some point during almost every meal, there are moments where one or all of us share our hearts. It happens naturally now and is a part of the rhythm of our meals. One day, we accidentally recorded 2½ minutes of conversation from our dinner via a voicemail on my phone. That recording is hilarious and definitely represents a Nunnery family dinner time very well as relationships are being strengthened through silly discourse that prepares each of us for more meaningful conversations.

- Sometimes Teach Them Diligently happens in the car if you are driving all over the place. Always be on the lookout for divine opportunities.

- Say goodbye to sleep when you have teens. Your room will become the gathering place . . . which is amazing! More times than I am able to recount, our teens have sat at the foot of our bed until the wee hours of the morning talking about what's on their heart. Those conversations are generally initiated by them as well, which defies the world's assertion that teenagers don't like talking to their parents. We have found that by listening to their thoughts and ideas when they were little, they believe their thoughts and ideas as teens are also important to us as well. Thus, they share, and we are able to shepherd their hearts through the trials and exciting new experiences that come with growing up.

- Make sure your child always knows exactly why he or she is being disciplined and then pray with your child after that time of discipline is finished. One mom shared, "I'll never forget one time my daughter threw her little arms around my neck after she was punished, and she said, 'Now pray with me, Mama!'" Neither parent nor child want to leave that moment with a fractured relationship. Grant forgiveness, reach out and hug them to physically bring them back into fellowship with you. Praying with them about what they've done wrong and asking God to help them choose to do right the next time is a great way to reinforce the ultimate authority in their life.

- One mom mentioned utilizing what she calls "Friday boxes" to help her children focus on the little things that God gives us and that bring us joy each week. As you recount each little thing, the faith of your children can certainly be strengthened. More details about this idea can be found at https://gypsyroadschool.blogspot.com/2017/01/friday-im-in-love-cure.

- Another mom told me about an idea for helping our littles form good helping habits and build character. "Hands are for helping character training" can be found at https://www.laramolettiere.com/hands-are-for-helping-character/.

- One family recounted what they call "Praise & Prayer," which they do almost every night. It's a time where they always share praise and prayer requests and often a BIBLE study will precede this. They went on to note that this tradition has kept their family close during some really tough times the past several years. (Once again, we see the promised blessing of raising children of promise!)

- Several moms told how they use Christmas cards from the family and bind them to make a prayer book. Then, throughout the year, they pray through the book, one family a week, on repeat until they make a new book the next year. It's a great idea to try to contact the family and ask for specific requests for that week too, for it not only lets them know you are praying for them but it also may give them a great idea to start within their own family.

- One year of dinner table devotions and discussion starters by Nancy Guthrie has been a great resource noted by some other Teach Them Diligently families.[1]

- One family noted that when their family started reading through the Word together in chronological order, things began to change. It may not sound like anything radical, but starting from the beginning and walking your way through God's Word, at your own pace, allowing for questions and study time, truly can be a game changer for your family.

- There are many families who utilize Prayer Jars and Blessing Jars. They write prayer requests on a sheet of paper and date it, then put them in the jar. Each day they take them out and read them and pray over them. When a prayer is answered, they date it and place it in the Blessing Jar. Periodically, they get all the blessings and answered prayers out and read those as a reminder that God is still working and still answering prayers!

- Sharing what you are thankful for that day during family devotion in the evenings is another great way to cultivate hearts that are attune to seeing God at work all around them. Around Thanksgiving you can start a thankful paper chain, add to it daily, then wrap it around your tree to create a Christmas tree of thanksgiving. That takes our eyes off of what we want and keeps us grateful for what God blesses us with daily.

- One mom noted that "The child-training and virtue-training Bible" has made disciplining with the Word easier because there is an easy-to-use index at your fingertips.

- Reading Christian books like *Grandpa's Box*, Chuck Black's the Kingdom Series,[2] and others aloud with our children allow us to present them the story of God's redemption through stories they can immediately relate with. It's a lot like Jesus' use of parables, teaching lessons through telling stories. Plus, reading aloud as a family is a great way to build memories and strengthen relationships with your children.

- One mom told me that when her now grown son was younger, she took a Shepherd's School Class called "Bible Omnibus" with him. That class gave them a framework of Bible themes to discuss, plus provided a great time of bonding with just him.

- Our friends at Mission-Minded Families offer some very helpful family discipleship courses with videos and worksheets for both children and teens. Learn about them at http://missionmindedfamilies. org/p/3-d-free and http://missionmindedfamilies. org/p/rock-solid.

- Traveling together is a great means to experience life in new and exciting ways together, and to help your children get a better view of just how big God and His plan for us really is.

- "Inspect what you expect." That was a phrase shared with me years ago and has definitely altered the way I parent since then. When I don't follow up on the things I ask my children to do, they get the idea that they don't really have to. I am shirking my responsibility in the training process and missing out on a chance to praise them for a job well done or to correct little things that need improvement. I also find that when I discover a task undone much later, I am more inclined to anger. As parents, it behooves us to follow up with our children, so they will know that we actually mean what we say and their obedience is expected and appreciated.

• A friend of mine shared something a bit unusual that they do in their home. They share everything. Whether it's a toy, clothing, office supplies, food, blankets, anything. Each child has only one item (a "special" blankie, lambie, and baby doll) that belongs to them. They are teaching that they only have any material item because God has allowed them to. This helps our children learn to view all the "stuff" as God's, and it will develop an overarching philosophy of sharing everything with others — in and out of your house.

• One mom noted how she has been encouraging her children to pray ESPECIALLY in those moments when they feel they are losing control over themselves. They are all believers, so they are all plugged in to that special power that comes only through the Holy Spirit! She noted that she reminds them of this and encourages them to ask God to give them power over the situation and help dealing with it, and help dealing with themselves. So, each of my boys has spent a lot of time alone in their room praying lately. It's especially amazing when I suggest prayer to one of them in the moment and they say, "I already did." She encourages us all by closing with, "We rub off on them, mamas!

Our words really aren't being ignored, even when it seems our kids do nothing but ignore us!"

✦ ✦ ✦ ✦

These great ideas from other discipleship-focused parents are meant to help you start formulating your own specific tips and ideas about how you can approach your children in order to reach their hearts and minds. There is certainly no end to the great ideas that have been tried and tested by God's families all around you, so I encourage you to find godly mentors at your church or in your community. Make it a priority to head to conferences like Teach Them Diligently and others where you will be surrounded by thousands of families who are also seeking to build disciple-making relationships with their children just like you are, and where you can learn from them and others who are further along in their parenting journey than you are. We were made to live in fellowship with one another, and there is much to learn from and to pass on to others when we do.

Endnotes:
1. Nancy Guthrie, *One Year of Dinner Table Devotions and Discussion Starters: 365 Opportunities to Grow Closer to God as a Family* (Carol Stream, IL: Tyndale Momentum, 2008).
2. Chuck Black, http://perfect-praise.com/; Grandpa's Box, http://teachthemdiligently.christianbook.com/grandpas-retelling-the-biblical-story-redemption/starr-meade/9780875528663/pd/52866X-?event=ESRCG.

About the Author

Leslie Nunnery is the co-founder of Teach Them Diligently Convention along with her husband, David. She is the homeschool mother of four children who range in age from 11–18. God has given her a strong burden to minister to Christian families to help support, encourage, and equip them to disciple their children, protect their marriages, and serve God in the ways He has planned for them. She is an advocate of home education with a strong focus on discipleship, which is evidenced in her writings and the events her family produces. She is also heavily involved in mission endeavors through Worldwide Tentmakers, for which her husband serves as president and which Teach Them Diligently supports.

Leslie Nunnery

The Nunnery family

THE WORLD NEEDS HOMESCHOOLERS
WHO ARE WILLING TO **LIVE BOLDLY.**

Living out the Gospel is like going against the cultural grain of the World. So we want to help! We're building a community that offers support, encouragement, experience, tools and resources all focused on you, and what you need each week as a homeschooling parent. New videos every week. Access to hundreds of audio sessions. Live online meetups and a community of supporting families. Come find wisdom and help!

Join us for 1-month for FREE (no obligation to stay) by using the promocode: **DILIGENTBOOK**

Are you ready to live boldly? Visit:
TeachThemdDiligently.net/365
and sign up today!

YOUR OPINION MATTERS

Your comments about this book are very helpful to others seeking resources on this topic.

Please consider reviewing this title at **Amazon.com**, **Christianbook.com** and **MasterBooks.com**.

Don't forget to recommend the book to your friends on Facebook , Twitter, & Pinterest too!

Thanks!

Tim Dudley
President & CEO
New Leaf Publishing Group